SELLING TO
HEROES VILLAINS
AND GEEKS

SELLING TO HEROES VILLAINS AND GEEKS

AN INSIDER'S GUIDE FOR NEW ANIME VENDORS

JILL M LEWIS

Publisher: Anime Vendor

Fort Lauderdale, FL

2015

DISCLAIMER

Readers of this book are advised to do their own due diligence when it comes to making business decisions. The author is not responsible for the success or failure of business decisions relating to any information presented in this book.

This book is presented solely for entertainment purposes. This book is designed to provide information on how to become a vendor at anime, comic and sci-fi conventions only. This information is provided and sold with the knowledge that the author does not offer any legal or other professional advice. If you need any such expertise, consult with the appropriate professional. This book does not contain all the information available on the subject. This book has not been created to be specific to any individual's or organization's situation or needs.

Every effort has been made to make this book as accurate as possible. However, there may be typographical and/or content errors. Therefore, this book should serve only as a general guide and not as the ultimate source of subject information. This book contains information that might be dated and is intended only to educate and entertain. The author shall have no liability or responsibility to any person or entity regarding any loss or damage incurred, or alleged to have been incurred, directly or indirectly, through the information contained in this book.

This book lists URLs or addresses to other websites. The URL or website address is provided for informational purposes only and does not constitute the endorsement of any products or services provided by the website. The URLs are subject to change, expire, or redirect without any notice. The author has not received any commission or fee to promote these websites. While the author takes no responsibility for the business practices of these companies and/or the performance of any product or service, the author has used some of the products or services and makes a recommendation in good faith based on that experience.

This book has been published by Anime Vendor. No part of this book may be reproduced in any form or by any means without the express written permission of the author. This includes reprints, excerpts, photocopying, recording or any future means of reproducing text. Please do not post this book or the information it contains on the Internet. If you think the information is valuable, please direct your family and friends to the place that you purchased your copy.

All trademarks and registered trademarks appearing in this book are the property of their respective owners. This book identifies product names and services known to be trademarks, registered trademarks or service marks of their respective holders. They are used throughout this book in an editorial fashion only. The use of a term in this book should not be regarded as affecting the validity of any trademark, registered trademark or service mark. The images remain under the copyright of the owners.

Readers agree to be bound by this disclaimer and copyright notice or otherwise may request a refund within five days of purchase. To request a refund, please send an email to jill@animevendor.com and include your name, mailing address, telephone number, date of purchase and digital copy of your receipt. A refund will be issued within thirty days.

Cover art: © Robert Chang
Cover designed by Scarlett Rugers Design *scarlettrugers.com*
Biography portrait: © Michael Lenehan
© 2015 Jill M Lewis
Printed in the United States of America
ISBN Paperback: 978-0-9964536-0-8
LCCN: 2015908395
Publisher: Anime Vendor

ACKNOWLEDGEMENTS

To all the geeks, nerds, heroes and villains who live in secret and only emerge during anime, comic, horror and sci-fi conventions – thank you. Your passion and devotion bring laughter, amazement and vendor sales. I find all of you charming. Chatting about your costumes and favorite anime characters sustains me through the long dealer-room hours. Thank you.

I wish to personally thank Steven and Cheryl Hale for pushing me to write this book. A double shout out to Steven for designing the website.

I also want to thank a few other fabulous people for their inspiration and contributions to my knowledge. Thank you for helping to make this book happen.

BTL Collectibles Show

Thank you to the BTL Collectibles Show owner who always wants to remain anonymous yet is known by everyone on the convention circuit. Heck, I met you the very first time we were both vendors at the same convention and here you are being acknowledged in my book. Psst ... anonymity is not in your DNA. Thank you for sharing over twenty years of knowledge on conventions and graciously agreeing to my multiple interview requests both on and off camera.

BTL Collectibles Show is South Florida's only monthly show where you can buy, sell and trade comics, toys, anime, manga, original artwork from comic book artists, sports cards, memorabilia, statues and much more!

Held monthly at Miccosukee Resort & Gaming
500 SW 177th Ave., Miami, FL 33194
facebook.com/btlshow
Dealer and show information: 305-710-6889

Silver Dragon Studio

Thank you to Thomas for reaching out and extending words of encouragement to a complete stranger. Your battle-tested advice is sprinkled throughout this book. The reader's startup prognosis is much brighter because of your contribution.

Owner: Thomas J Mulvey
Merchandise: Celtic, gothic, fantasy jewelry, custom leatherwork and imported merchandise from Alchemy Gothic of England.
Store Number: 571-263-9013
silverdragonstudio.net
facebook.com/pages/Silver-Dragon-StudioGothic-Bling/365196779124

TABLE OF CONTENTS

Selling to Heroes, Villains and Geeks 1
    So what's my backstory? 2
    The backstory of this book 3
The customer's backstory 6
    What about your backstory – vendor or artist? 8

PART 1: THE CARDINAL RULES 13
Cardinal rule 1: Customer Con 17
    Merchandising through your customer's eyes 19
    Customer preferred categories 20
    Customer hot topics 24
    Customer pictionary 25
Cardinal rule 2: Variety is the spice of life 31
    Spice up your merchandise 32
    #JustTheRightSpice 37
Cardinal rule 3: Think different 41
    Dare to be different 42
    Unearthing unique items in a different country 47
Cardinal rule 4: Avoid customer price shock 55
    Pricing best practices 56
    The psychology of pricing 57
Cardinal rule 5: Ferocious bargain hunter 63
    Prowling for bargain prices 64
    Avoiding supplier hiccups 67
Cardinal rules wrap-up 69

PART 2: BUSINESS BATTLE PLAN BLUEPRINT 71

Laying the groundwork for your battle plan 75
ASSIGNMENT #1:
Conduct online research on what's hot and what's not 76
ASSIGNMENT #2:
Ferret out popular merchandise through fieldwork 78
ASSIGNMENT #3:
Build variety into your merchandise plan 81
ASSIGNMENT #4:
Google search the Japanese names of anime 84

The hunt for merchandise 87
ASSIGNMENT #5:
Find unique items on Japanese sites 89
ASSIGNMENT #6:
Master the Japanese auction bidding process 95
ASSIGNMENT #7:
Understand the Japanese proxy service purchasing
process and fees 100
ASSIGNMENT #8:
Understand the Japanese proxy service shipping
process and fees 106
ASSIGNMENT #9:
Price your merchandise to sell fast 110
ASSIGNMENT #10:
Investigate Chinese wholesalers 115

The nuts and bolts of your battle plan 121
ASSIGNMENT #11:
Craft your merchandise plan 122
ASSIGNMENT #12:
Create your business battle plan 125

PART 3: INITIATE LAUNCH SEQUENCE 133

Convention road map 137
   The road to vendor registration 143
Convention logbook 147
   The 'L' Word 147
   Pre-convention planning dispatch checklist 154
   Last minute, nitty-gritty details 156
Where's Superman when you need him? 159
   Booth setups 159

A behind-the-scenes peek at my booth 164
The most popular booth in the aisle......................................168
The moment of truth..**173**
Manage your customer service moments......................... 174
Good and bad convention moments 177
Financially naked **181**

SELLING TO HEROES, VILLAINS AND GEEKS – THE FINALE 187

Appendices: Vendor's Grab Bag..**191**
Appendix 1: Trusted suppliers..192
Appendix 2: Sample vendor application............................194
Illustration and Photo Credits **200**
Honorable Mentions **201**

SELLING TO HEROES, VILLAINS AND GEEKS

ANIME AND MANGA CONVENTIONS (CONS) are morphing into major pop culture events in cities across the country. Small and large cons are merging comics, anime, manga, video games, toys, movies, sci-fi, horror, wrestling (WWE), supernatural, paranormal and fantasy into one big, multi-genre affair. Nowadays even traditional Comic Cons, originally made popular by die-hard comic book fans, cast a wider net to compete with their pop culture brethren. Not content with this range of genres, all cons are spreading their tentacles to include gothic, steampunk, Japanese fashion and magic, plus anything else remotely connected to a main theme. If convention organizers think fans are interested in something, they'll simply tack it on to their laundry list of themes.

Conventions are thriving because they dramatically ratchet up the fans' enjoyment of anime and manga. They shift the entertainment from the movie, computer and television screen into the real world where fans can touch, feel, socialize and interact at every level. Cons specialize in bringing to life and celebrating popular and classic anime shows. They also showcase and create buzz around new series and upcoming movie releases. There are sneak previews, premiers, panel discussions and celebrity guest appearances. Cons are so popular that all artists working in the industry will jump at the chance to book an appearance as a celebrity guest.

And the fans – geeks, nerds and under-the-radar admirers – absolutely love the convention-provided opportunity to meet the celebrities and the behind-the-scenes professionals of each genre. Fans come face-to-face with the people they idolize and follow on Twitter, Facebook and Instagram. They get to ask them questions, take pictures and acquire their autographs – all for a fee, of course.

But there's much more. The vendors provide all of the sought-after anime and comic merchandise that attendees scramble to purchase. At large conventions, fans dart among the different vendors occupying over one thousand booth spaces, not including the independent artists selling handmade creations. Fans with cash in hand spend liberally and the vendors, the smart ones, can rack up sales in excess of several thousand dollars over one weekend.

So how do you get started as a vendor? What should you sell? What are the risks? Will you fail miserably? Can you eke out a living? Can you quit your job and still live comfortably? What information do you need? Where are the freakin' books and blog posts on this subject? You can't sign up for a class, get a degree, watch a webinar or even find a decent YouTube video on this topic. But don't fret, that's where this book comes in.

Selling to Heroes, Villains and Geeks will guide you through the process of becoming a vendor. It is a guide, not a system, and it is definitely not a 'get rich quick scheme.' *Selling to Heroes, Villains and Geeks* eliminates most of the guesswork by pointing out things you need to investigate and spotlighting areas you didn't even know were part of the start-up process.

So what's my backstory?

Growing up, I always thought having mutant powers would be the best gift ever. Never mind the distrust from the non-mutants, the hours of training to master my powers, or the fear of going over to the dark side – mutant powers would be a cinch to handle. Heck, *X-Men's* Storm manages it just fine.

Alas, no mutant powers ever materialized. But I did discover my power to earn an MBA from

Columbia University and turn into a high-performance marketer. Mere mortals, such as myself, could change the future with smart, creative, customer-focused marketing plans. For twenty-five years, I've launched products that have rocketed to success, developed memorable advertising campaigns, and guided businesses that have generated hundreds of millions of dollars in annual sales. And I went on to fly all over the world without the assistance of any mutant powers. I conducted business in London, Paris, Frankfurt, Geneva, Milan, Tokyo, São Paulo, Beijing, Hamburg, Barcelona, Johannesburg, Toronto, Mexico City, Prague and almost every state in the US.

For the past several years, I have been using my marketing powers to vend at anime, comic and sci-fi conventions. My customers are heroes, villains and geeks who use their creative powers to bring their favorite characters to life with a little help from my merchandise. I know what piques their interest and opens their wallets or purses. I can even get their Moms and Dads to pitch in several bucks – it's not easy being the parent of heroes and villains. And all of this has helped me to become a strikingly-successful vendorpreneur (think vendor plus entrepreneur).

Selling to Heroes, Villains and Geeks is based on my experience of becoming a vendor and selling products at anime and manga conventions. I've covered everything, and I do mean e-v-e-r-y-t-h-i-n-g, you need to know to move from 'I think I want to do this' to 'I can barely hold back my excitement to vend at my first convention and sell something to my very first customer!'

The backstory of this book

This book's backstory begins at my vendor booth. Imagine this: 43,000 attendees, 210 vendors, 158 artists and 250 celebrity guests packed into the Miami Beach Convention Center for a comic book, anime, animation, video game, fantasy, sci-fi and pop culture convention. At the end of the second day, one inquisitive couple approached my vendor booth wanting to know the ins and outs of becoming a vendor. I was tired, the bones in my right foot were aching and the dealers' area had just closed for the evening. The convention staff was clearing the exhibition hall of last-minute shoppers and preparing to secure the room for the night. Big security guards were becoming less and less friendly with the stragglers and the lights were dimming inside the hall. But despite this, I answered the couple's questions for about an hour.

This is when I realized that there is just no information out there to help people start their own vendor businesses. New vendors are forced to jump in the deep end with no life preserver and just pray for the best. So the idea for *Selling to Heroes, Villains and Geeks* was born. This book is your life preserver. It will help you drive your vendor plans forward with my hard-earned, unfiltered advice, and step-by-step instructions that frame the make-or-break decisions in the vendor business.

I'll answer all of the crucial questions about merchandise, including what to sell and where to buy. Each chapter reveals answers to your questions through a combination of information about what works and what doesn't, detailed instructions and examples. You'll complete work assignments to help you get started and I've included color images and photos to make sure your mental picture of the information provided matches real-world situations. We cover all this in three easy-to-follow parts:

Part 1: The cardinal rules share the foundational principles of vending at conventions. This will give you all of the critical marketing knowledge you need before embarking on your vendor business. These rules are tested, tried and infallible!

Part 2: Business battle plan blueprint shows you how to do what you need to do and puts you in the driver's seat to craft your business strategy. We'll answer the cut-through questions of prime importance to your business and merchandise strategies. You'll build your battle business plan, hands-on, by practicing everything you learned in *Part 1*.

Part 3: Initiate launch sequence marches you through the final steps of launching your business. We drop you off at your first convention prepared and ready to attract a slew of customers. You will be all set for a fast, money-making start at your first convention.

You'll find 'Sensei tips' sprinkled throughout the book that share the insider secrets you won't find anywhere else. There are also 'Oops alerts' that point out regrettable new-vendor decisions that led to disastrous sales results (names have been omitted in these to protect their identities). The 'Oops alerts' point out some of the more head-scratching new-vendor *faux pas* I witness over and over again, so look for these in the coming chapters.

Selling to Heroes, Villains and Geeks delivers premium business information garnered from years of experience. You can short-circuit the new-venture learning curve and use this book's blueprint to launch your foray into the vending business. This book will save you endless hours of Google searches, looking for answers that are just not there. I have written this book specifically to give new vendors all of the answers and advice they need to get started – it's all right here!

If you have any questions while you are reading this book, you are welcome to send me an email or visit my Facebook page to find out my next convention appearance. I'll be happy to talk to you! Reach out to jill@animevendor.com or facebook.com/animevendor.

But remember that, while this book will prepare you, in the end it's up to you. Your passion, drive, willingness to learn and perseverance will be what pushes you to the other side – the vendor side of the dealer-room doors. And once you get to the other side, the customers will be the lifeblood of your business. Learning about why they attend conventions, what they want and what can surprise and delight them is fundamental to your success. To be successful, you have to get inside your customer's head and learn their backstory.

THE CUSTOMER'S BACKSTORY

CONVENTIONS ARE NOT YOUR NORMAL weekend activity such as going to the beach, a club or out to dinner. They're like going to the movies but then stepping inside the movie screen and becoming a part of the action. It's no wonder that cons are so popular.

At cons, attendees are free to let their imaginations and creativity loose. They get the chance to role-play their favorite characters in an environment where that is celebrated and encouraged. They painstakingly make costumes to wear at the con (half-naked is acceptable, although PG-13 is requested). Fellow-con goers notice and compliment their costume creations. Prior to the convention, role-players are generally anonymous fans, but the moment they show up in costume, they are among other fans and are in high demand. They are asked over and over again to pose for pictures. They can barely make it from the parking lot to the registration desk without being swamped by numerous picture requests and they eagerly agree, enjoying the attention. Accepting the compliments and posing for the camera, you can see the sparkle in their facial expressions and dispositions.

Fans turn up on opening day full of enthusiasm and flush with money. Lines stretch down the hall and around the corner waiting for the convention's dealer room to open. Discovering what the room holds is just as exciting as meeting the guest celebrities. They wonder what mystery and delight hides behind those doors. They gawk at their watches, waiting for the moment the doors will swing open. Their hearts pound and their anticipation is full throttle. Fans at the head of the line strain their necks to peek inside every time security opens the doors to grant the VIP ticket holders their early entrance.

Con attendees know that inside the dealer room there exists must-have-or-I'll-die merchandise from their favorite manga, anime, sci-fi or horror series. And when the doors finally open for general admission, their frenzied search will begin. They dash from vendor to vendor squealing with excitement as they stumble across items that make their heart beat faster. Their screams echo across the room for other vendors and attendees to hear.

Over the course of the convention, tens of thousands of attendees will pour through the exhibit hall, eyeing and buying merchandise from their favorite anime or manga series. Whether conventions last one, two, three or four days, attendees will browse the dealer room, chat with the vendors and track down the perfect item.

The convention's atmosphere sparks emotional highs for the attendees and they tend to develop an emotional attachment to their dealer-room purchases. Their joy may appear over-the-top, but you have to remember that they're in an over-the-top environment. I mean, Darth Vader is walking around, for heaven's sake!

The emotional crescendo builds with each item bought. Their discoveries and prized purchases present another opportunity to be noticed by other attendees. People want to know which vendor sells which item and where their booth is located. Getting asked questions like this by their peers is confirmation of their smart purchasing decision. And if the lucky purchaser is able to say, 'I bought the last one' – Bingo! They have something special that others want but no one else can get. Can you imagine the smile on their face? You'll see this all the time if you're a vendor that sells unique or exclusive items.

The more you can get inside the attendee's head, the better your merchandise purchasing decisions will be. Instinctively, you'll know what will appeal to your customers and which items you should quickly bypass. Your merchandise selection may only include items created by others or you may decide to tap into your inner artist and sell your own handmade creations. So next up is the existential question: who am I?

What about your backstory – vendor or artist?

The first decision you need to make is whether you are going to sell as a vendor or an artist at conventions. You need to make this decision before going any further because it will affect what you can and can't sell and therefore your entire business strategy. Before you answer, it helps to understand the definitions of both and how they differ in terms of selling at cons.

Selling as an Artist

Artists sell or promote their own personal work. This classification includes independent publishers, crafts people, indie developers, filmmakers, writers and entrepreneurs, such as users of etsy.com, pinterest.com and deviantart.com. As an artist, you can sell anything as long as you made it. However, you *may not* sell merchandise that was not created by your own hands.

Beautifully-designed artist table with the talented Krystal Alexander, dressed as Amy Pond from the series Dr. Who

Artists are assigned a table in what is generally referred to as Artist Alley and pay substantially lower registration fees than vendors. Artist Alley can be located in the hallways or corridors of the convention site, within the dealer room or on a separate floor, which may make it seem like you're in

Siberia. Some conventions make a conscious effort to locate artists in a prime location, while others shove them off to the side.

Often out in the open at smaller conventions, Artist Alley is not secured overnight. Artists must remove their merchandise at the end of each day to avoid theft. This means you'll have to re-setup each day of the convention.

Selling as a vendor

Vendors can sell anything they want. Also referred to as dealers or exhibitors, vendors are allowed to sell items created by a third party and manufactured commercially as well as their own personal works of art or other handmade items. Their merchandise doesn't even have to be related to the convention theme. If it's legal, they can sell it.

Standard 10' x 10' vendor booth

Vendors are located in the dealer room or exhibit hall, which is typically separate from Artist Alley (which can get pretty lonely the farther away it is from the dealer room). Also, the dealer room is locked overnight, meaning vendors only have to set up once per convention.

Artists are not excluded from participating as vendors. You just have to register as a vendor and pay the substantially-higher fee. You may be asking yourself, 'Why would an artist do that?' Well, the dealer-room foot traffic surpasses Artist Alley by a sizeable amount so it definitely increases your exposure and can help with sales. You can also take advantage of the vendor rules and sell both your own work at the same time as selling retail merchandise, therefore, increasing overall sales. Also, vendor booths are much larger than the spaces assigned to artists and vendors can purchase as many booths as they want. Many conventions limit artists to one 6' or 8' table and, in some cases, just half of a table.

Celebrity tables for photo-ops and autograph signings are located in the dealer room. The scheduled events are held near or inside the exhibit hall. Television stations frequently shoot convention footage about the dealers and their merchandise. Artists who want to be in the thick of it will often register as a vendor so they can secure a high traffic booth location.

 Sensei Tip: Budget-constrained artists should try to partner with vendors as worker bees to score prime space inside the dealer room. Space is set aside at the vendor's booth for the artist's items, and the artist helps to sell both the vendor's items and their own creations. The vendor pays most, if not all, of the vendor registration fees.

This raises another important question: Is it better to sell handmade items or retail merchandise, like figures and plushies? Well, if you want to tap into a redonkulously-massive pool of potential buyers, you'll want to go the retail route.

For example, we all know *Batman* – the dark knight. Batman's fan base reaches the stratosphere. So, naturally, *Batman* merchandise outsells handmade items from unknown individual artists at conventions.

| *Merchandise* | *Pool of Potential Buyers* |

Artist handmade items

Commercial items based on anime series, movies, manga publications, and video games

This book will focus on successfully selling commercially-manufactured retail items as a vendor. However, even if you're an artist, writer or craftsperson, a sizeable chunk of this information is also applicable to your business. In fact, whether you are planning on registering as an artist or a vendor, if you absorb all of the information in this book, your convention business will be profitable right from the start.

Author note: Throughout the book, the word vendor is interchangeable with the words exhibitor or dealer. The use of the word anime refers to anime TV shows. Manga describes a Japanese comic book or graphic novel.

PART 1:

THE CARDINAL RULES

You probably already have potential merchandise ideas swirling around in your mind. *Stop!* Before you carve your merchandise plan in stone, it is well worth learning the cardinal rules. Each rule is a minefield of information that must be understood by everyone contemplating becoming a vendor.

These rules form the bedrock of every successful vendor business. We will weave our way through the five rules over the next several chapters. And remember, these cardinal rules of business are apropos to both vendors and artists. Here's what's in store:

- **Cardinal rule 1: Customer Con**
  As a vendor, your focus has to be on the customer and giving them what they want. To quote P&G, 'The customer is boss.' Fans won't purchase items because you love the stuff you're selling. They want items from anime and manga *they* love. Duh!

- **Cardinal rule 2: Variety is the spice of life**
  You need to carry items from several different anime because your customers love more than one anime series. They'll be avid followers of many shows and will fall in love with a variety of human and nonhuman characters.

- **Cardinal rule 3: Think different**
  Make sure you sell unique and exclusive items not carried by other vendors. Double duh! Convention-goers are magnetically pulled to vendors with exclusive, unique or cutting-edge merchandise.

- **Cardinal rule 4: Avoid customer price shock**
  Do not overprice your items. Attendees set spending limits and vendors, artists and celebrity guests are all vying for a share of the attendee's budget.

- **Cardinal rule 5: Ferocious bargain hunter**
  Purchase items at a deep discount and sell at a higher price. This fundamental principle for generating eye-popping profit works flawlessly if the other cardinal rules are also practiced.

Rookie vendors often unwittingly choose what I call 'the doomsday plan' because they either overlook or ignore the cardinal rules. Regrettably, they fail miserably because they don't grasp one or more of these essential rules.

You might be thinking, 'Ok, that's great, rules are good. But I need specifics on how to execute these ideas.' Well, keep reading – it's all included in this book.

We need to cover the cardinal rules first so you can implement these as a part of your business plan. Then we'll get right into the step-by-step instructions on how to put the cardinal rules into action in *Part 2: Business battle plan blueprint*. Then in *Part 3: Initiate launch sequence,* we cover the remaining details to get your business off to a fast start. And by fast, I mean profitable. You'll find numerous real-life vendor examples laced throughout this book, both their good decisions and some that were not so good.

So let's move right along into our first cardinal rule. This rule shines a light on the items customers want and frequently purchase at conventions.

CARDINAL RULE 1: CUSTOMER CON

IT DOESN'T MATTER IF YOU'RE vending at Comic Con, Super Con, Mega Con or any other con, it's always 'Customer Con' for vendors. While the customer backstory exposed the emotional component of the convention experience for attendees, this cardinal rule is all about what the customer wants to buy.

The attendees need to be your sole focus and what merchandise they want is what's important. You'll uncover this through research and hard work – not guesswork. However, too many new vendors make the critical mistake of selling merchandise they love and expect convention attendees to love it too. Or they offer merchandise they *think* is going to be a hot-seller based on their own personal taste instead of what the customer truly wants. This is where pride and lack of research can cost new vendors lots of money.

Etch this in your brain: It's not about what you like. I understand that most vendors get involved in cons because they love anime or manga as much as the attendees. And every vendor has their personal favorite anime. But you're not selling to yourself; you're selling to other people. You need to stock items that the convention attendees want to purchase. Period. Enter *Cardinal rule 1: Customer Con*. Make sure you're selling merchandise customers want. You're laughing, right? You're thinking, 'This is too obvious.' But just wait until you read about new vendors who arrived at a con supremely confident that they had merchandise customers would want to buy – and were wrong.

Every dealer room has its share of vendors who can't seem to sell anything – all weekend. I've seen instances where no one, not one single person, was interested in their merchandise. I've seen vendors take naps at their booths during three-day conventions because there was nothing else for them to do. These vendors didn't do their homework. They guessed at what the customer wanted and they got it wrong. As you can understand, a bad show for a new vendor can completely crush their spirit. They leave the convention utterly defeated.

Attendees will always purchase merchandise that appeals to them emotionally. They bypass products that don't. Merchandise from their favorite anime, comic, sci-fi, horror and paranormal series stirs up feelings of excitement. And the vendors who sell it enjoy crazy-mad foot traffic. The vendors who don't, don't. Attendees know exactly what they want and if you're not selling their favorite items, they'll get them from another vendor.

Let's dissect one vendor's merchandise selection at a one-day comic book convention I stopped by recently. This vendor was attempting to sell chess sets where the game was played using magic cards. Can you immediately spot the problem? Besides the issue that only chess players would be interested, perhaps the bigger problem was the amount of time needed to explain the concept to anyone who happened to show interest. I hung out for a few hours in the dealer room and guess how much he sold? Nada. Hmm, that vendor's merchandise selection boggles the mind. Did I mention the convention was a comic book memorabilia show?

The core problem was that he tried to sell items he was in love with. He was a chess player and clearly loved magic. But no one else did. Alas, selling chess sets played with magic cards as his only merchandise flunks cardinal rule 1 (and a few more to boot). For him, this was a financially-painful strikeout.

Sensei tip: Artists need to take careful note here. You are especially susceptible to failure in this way. The painful truth is that attendees aren't automatically drawn to your artistic style or premade art like they are to merchandise from their favorite anime.

According to the Census Bureau and Bureau of Labor Statistics, twenty-five percent of startup businesses fail in the first year. Thirty-six percent fail in the second and forty-four percent don't survive beyond the third year.

You will avoid this fate because you're going to do something that they didn't do – research. You're already learning a valuable rule about what it takes to be successful in vending.

You might feel a little deflated at this point because, like most new vendors, you were planning to start your business with what you know and love. Chin up! Maybe only some minor adjustments are necessary. Or, you may have to rethink your whole plan. But it will be worth it in the long run.

Let's get started with what you need to do so that you are giving customers exactly what *they* want!

Merchandising through your customer's eyes

Fact: Customers want merchandise related to the convention's theme. Fans register to attend a convention because the theme, the celebrity guests and the activities appeal to them. A book fair attracts people interested in books. An anime convention attracts people interested in anime.

Vendors who sell all-natural wraps to tighten or tone your skin, or beautiful, decorative warmers that melt scented wax using a light bulb, or chair massages won't find any customers at an anime, paranormal and horror convention. These vendors are trying to target adults who, at a different time and place, may be prime prospects, but it's *Batman*, *The Walking Dead* and *My Little Pony* that occupy the interest of attendees at a convention. This mismatch of convention theme and merchandise happens far too often and I witness it at almost every convention.

Oops alert: Colleges often set up tables at conventions as a strategy to reach young adults. But they quickly figure out the fans are preoccupied with cosplaying and meeting celebrities. They aren't thinking about their education! Like clockwork, the college staff depart midway through the first day, leaving literature and handouts on their table. They had the right target market, but the wrong time.

Be smart and adjust your merchandise to align with the convention's theme. Take cues from the media, comic, anime or TV celebrities that are headlining the con you are vending at. Fans love to get autographs on merchandise from their favorite shows or characters. Also, any anime that is still rolling out new episodes or releasing full-length movies will generate strong fan interest and, consequently, the demand for its merchandise will be sky high.

By looking through your customers' eyes, you can correctly tailor your merchandise so that they pay attention to your booth. Then note what they purchase to get even more cues to the types of items and categories that are attracting the most interest.

Customer preferred categories

Fact: Attendees consistently purchase certain types of items at conventions. Favorites include figures, plushies, artwork, wall scrolls, posters, comic books and cosplay accessories like key chains, pocket watches and swords. There are just certain categories of merchandise that are top sellers at every con.

In the words of Lord Alfred Tennyson, 'Ours not to reason why, ours but to do and [make money].' Okay, maybe those weren't his exact words, but you get the idea. I have no special insight into *why* certain categories are in higher demand at conventions than others, but I do know *what* they are. And the toy manufacturers also know what they are and concentrate on releasing the most merchandise in these categories. So, what are the popular categories?

Knowing the bestselling merchandise categories is one thing, but the devil is most definitely in the detail with con attendees. However, this is a good start. Things outside of these categories will be slow-sellers or, worse, non-sellers. So strike them from your merchandise plan. Let's dive into the popular categories a bit further so you get a better feel for the kind of merchandise you might stock at your booth. These particular items are consistently the most frequently purchased at cons:

- **Figures** are quite possibly the bestselling items at conventions and among all toys worldwide. Japanese manga and anime producers churn out a figure for every recurring character. Outside anime, every single television show, movie or entertainment event (like WWE) also rushes to release figures of their stars. Why? Because the fans want them.

  Customers tend to prefer figure sizes that are 1-2 inches, 5-7 inches and 9-10 inches. Prices for these generally fall within the $6 to $60 range but can extend to several hundred dollars. Many figures are released as collectible limited editions or can turn into valuable collectibles over time.

*Fullmetal Alchemist. Alphonse Elric
Medicom Figure, value tripled in less than a year*

  The list of companies releasing figures is too numerous to expound and not important at this juncture. Just know that it's hard to go wrong if you include figures in your merchandise plan.

- **Plushies** are cute, soft and elicit lots of 'oohs' and 'aahs' from attendees. They serve to accessorize many cosplayers' outfits or become another cherished item in someone's bedroom collection. Plushies are easily one of the top-selling merchandise categories worldwide.

The most popular sizes are 3-4 inches, 7-8 inches and 12-14 inches. Most convention prices fall within the $8 to $40 range. The entertainment companies behind every anime series that lasts more than a hot second pump out plushies resembling its human and non-human characters.**Art, posters and wall scrolls (fabric posters)** of anime characters, television celebrities and movie stars hang in the bedrooms of many fans. What fan doesn't want to stare at their favorite character every day? And vendors are happy to make their dreams come true.

Prices range from $8 to $20 (autograph not included) with many special offers from vendors such as 'Buy two for $20.' Wall scrolls or poster sizes are frequently referred to by a letter and number combination such as A4 or B6.

The following chart shows the most common sizes:

Size	*Width x Height (in)*	*Size*	*Width x Height (in)*
A0	33.1 × 46.8	B0	40.6 × 57.3
A1	23.4 × 33.1	B1	28.7 × 40.6
A2	16.5 × 23.4	B2	20.3 × 28.7
A3	11.7 × 16.5	B3	14.3 × 20.3
A4	8.3 × 11.7	B4	10.1 × 14.3
A5	5.8 × 8.3	B5	7.2 × 10.1
A6	4.1 × 5.8	B6	5.0 × 7.2

- **Manga or comics books are** *not b*ig sellers at multi-genre conventions. Seriously. They take up too much time to shop for. You see, ninety-nine percent of comic vendors stick multiple boxes containing 300 comic books per box on their tables. This is guaranteed to repel every attendee except the most die-hard of comic book fans. By the time a customer searches through two boxes, they've already looked at 600 comic books. Can you say 'brain overload?' These vendors are not merchandising through the customer's eyes.

Conventions schedule back-to-back and concurrent panel discussions, celebrity photo opportunities and autograph signings. Attendees just won't spend hours searching through thousands of comic books when they would rather stand in line for a celebrity photo-op or a panel discussion. The choice is obvious.

I don't want to completely trash comic book vendors because there are marketing savvy ones who create customer-friendly displays. They may customize $20 packets of comic books from popular genres (for example, vampires or zombies) and set up attractive display racks that draw sizeable customer traffic and plenty of sales.

- **Cosplay Accessories & Jewelry:** Key chains are another item frequently purchased at conventions. Everyone has keys and, therefore, everyone needs a key chain of some description. Every fan also has a backpack and these easily clip onto the shoulder straps. In fact, you'll see key chains in the most creative places on the attendees' bodies because, of course, other fans must see them.

  Miniature figures, plushies or charms are the draw for these items. Prices range from $8 to $18.

  Another popular accessory for both costumes and street clothes is pocket watches. They're shiny, cool and attendees love to pull them out of their pocket, flip open the lid and look at the time. This 'action' shows off their purchase to their friends. Convention prices range from $15 to $35.

  Like bees to honey, fans gobble up swords at conventions. These oversize props are the ultimate accessory to any costume. Their shape, awesome power, shift shaping abilities and life force are an integral part of many popular anime and manga series. A costume isn't complete until the fan is united with their character's weapon of choice. Convention prices range from $10 to $40.

The bottom line is that merchandise purchased by anime fans is the engine behind dealer-room sales. Convention organizers strategically invite celebrity guests specifically to appeal to the anime fan base and to stack the deck for a profitable dealer room. And you need to stack the deck in your favor by zeroing in on items that are shoo-in top-sellers.

We've scratched the surface of what customers want; we still need to dive deeper. Popular items and the anime they're associated with are inseparable in the mind of the customer. For example, if a customer is searching for a *Psycho Pass* key chain, then they'll shun all other anime key chains. If they want a *Pokémon* Greninja plush, they'll ignore the 150 other *Pokémon* plushies for sale. So learning what anime is hot and what's not is the next step in stocking red-hot bestsellers.

Customer hot topics

Fact: Con attendees want to purchase items from massive runaway blockbuster hits *and* their favorite anime series. At conventions, you'll notice the top-selling items are from anime series that are growing in popularity in the US after already becoming a hit in Japan.

You need to stay up-to-date on popular shows in order to predict customer purchases. Since the heart of anime and manga beats in Japan, you'll want to start your search there. Proactively sniff out what the popular and trending new anime series are there, because the US will likely follow. A small word of caution, though – not all shows that are popular in Japan are automatic *bona fide hits* in the US. Stay clear of obscure series with tiny cult followings. The pool of potential buyers is too small to be worth your investment.

Also, keep abreast of classic anime reboots, current series storylines and next season's scheduled premieres. Relax! You don't have to watch all of them. There are resources to help you gauge fan interest in new and old anime shows. Convention goers, other vendors and American websites, like animenewsnetwork.com, are prime sources of information on what's hot and what's not. Also, Funimation (funimation.com) delivers the latest anime and manga news while also co-sponsoring numerous conventions.

There are instructions and assignments in *Part 2: Business battle plan blueprint* that show you how to research what's trending in anime and how to search and purchase items from those shows.

You'll quickly learn to speak 'anime' after a few website visits. And it's important to speak the language in order to converse with your customers. You do not want to seem clueless. Fans are more likely to buy from vendors who know what they're talking about and can share their enthusiasm. When you're up to date with the customer hot topics, you'll be credible, and able to do a better job convincing them to make a purchase.

Always remember that convention-goers are in pursuit of items from popular classics *and* trending new anime shows. By pairing the anime show with the right items, you'll position your business to ring up numerous sales over the course of a weekend. But who are these customers that can make you smile all weekend as they plunk down $10, $20 $40 or $80 at your booth?

Customer pictionary

Fact: Knowing and understanding the customers you are targeting is the overarching rule for a successful business. Vendors that possess knowledge about their customers and use it to their profitable advantage are wildly successful. Knowing specifically what their buyers want, savvy vendors carry merchandise that is guaranteed to catch their customer's eye.

You can't please every con attendee. But you need to know which customers you are targeting so that you can give them what they want. You'll get more specific in an assignment later in the book, but first let's take a stab at building the framework of a customer profile.

> In *Part 2: Business battle plan blueprint* you will specify exactly who you are targeting with your merchandise when you complete assignment #12.

Customer profiling may sound a bit like a mug shot lineup of your customers, but the goal is to provide a snapshot of the type of person you hope to attract. Do Aunt Molly and Cousin Fred really represent the customer who will make your business successful? No. So, profiling is vital. Done properly, it helps narrow down your merchandise decisions and keeps you from going astray when you're looking for ways to expand your product offering.

Every business can benefit from profiling their customers. The information you gather makes it easier to distinguish what it takes for customers to buy from you instead of other vendors. The more information you have about your customers, the easier it is to spot new merchandise opportunities. And you can tailor your merchandise based on their profiles.

The first step to take when assembling your customer profile is to create broad descriptions of various target customers. I'm talking about a high-level view including demographic data (age, gender or race) and other personal information such as interests, activities and opinions. The latter is referred to as psychographics; what you're seeking is what the customer wants and why, how they carry out their everyday life, what they value, and, most importantly, how they make choices when it comes to what they purchase. Re-read the customer backstory. It is fertile ground for beginning to develop your target's psychographics.

Sensei tip: Kids under twelve years old are not your target customers. They are under strict supervision from their parents. They can typically buy one item and one item only. Generous parents may set the budget at twenty dollars, but others limit spending to much smaller amounts.

However, the parents of kids who get good grades will reward their young 'uns with a pretty big spending limit. I steer these kids toward my higher-priced items. How do I know which kids got the good grades? Their very proud parents boast about them as soon as they walk up to my booth. I consider these purchases bonus sales since I'm not actively targeting kids.

One of your more profitable demographic targets is dads with their teenage daughters. These lovely individuals are more than happy to buy their princesses whatever they want. No spending limits!

The second step is to divide your customers into groups or segments that have similar wants. Segmenting customers is important because it helps you to identify the different wants of different groups. For example, you can segment your customers by merchandise category, price point, anime shows and genre. A typical customer segment could be described as follows:

customers who purchase *figures* priced between $20 and $80 are eighteen years to thirty-five-years old, and include both men and women. They like beautifully-detailed figures, limited editions, or figures no longer in wide distribution and most likely won't take the figure out of the box. You might also have a segment interested in figures that are $14 or less. This segment will handle the figure frequently and care more about its functionality and being able to play with the item. Both segments' psychographics overlap because of their desire for figures representing what's currently smoking hot in anime, TV and new movie releases.

Targeting customers by segment makes it easier to make sure you're carrying the appropriate merchandise for those customers. Spoiler alert: The next cardinal rule discusses in depth the need for carrying a variety of merchandise versus opting for one type of item or focusing on only one anime show. But variety is only effective if it meets the needs of the different customer segments you've identified as your targets.

The third step is to virtually meet your customer. Find a picture of what you think your customers look like. Turning your collection of information into a real person allows you to visualize the type of merchandise that will appeal to them. Do I need to remind you that you are *not* in the customer target? To give you an idea of where to start, I classify my customers along these lines:

Window Shoppers   Target Customers

As I mentioned in the earlier 'Sensei tip', kids are not your target. Because of their parents' budget mandate, they'll window shop at your booth until their parents make them move on. This also means parents of kids twelve years and younger are not your target. They feed, clothe and put a roof over their kid's head and paid for them to come to the convention, so they only have a small budget for dealer room purchases. Also, older adults and grandparents fall into the window-shopper category. They want to and, most likely, will buy their grandchildren one item, but it won't be expensive. The cheaper, the better. They've bought their grandkids so much stuff since their birth, they're not looking to splurge. How do I know? They tell me. Customers are more than willing to share the thinking behind their purchases.

Fans eighteen years to thirty-five-years old are my bullseye target customers. When I merge their demographics and psychographics with my merchandise, I can develop a complete profile. For example, one of the popular categories I stock is plushies from the hot anime show and video game *Pokémon*. So, a customer profile for one of my target customer segments looks like this: anyone eighteen years to thirty-five-years old, wearing an elaborate costume, clothing with anime art or any type of costume accessory is a potential customer. They have a deep-seated love for *Pokémon* with an affinity for the legendary ones. These customers first began watching *Pokémon* when the first generation was popular many, many years ago. Their favorite *Pokémon* characters are now called legendary because many new generations have since been introduced into the series. Even though they no longer watch the TV show they are extremely active with the video game and they have up-to-the-minute knowledge of newly released *Pokémon*. They gravitate toward the bigger size plushies that are eleven to twenty inches tall and priced from twenty to sixty-five dollars. This profile, along with a mental picture of my customers, helps to tailor my decision on which *Pokémon* characters to stock.

Once you have visualized the type of customers you want to attract and researched the items that are popular, you are ready to plan your merchandise strategy in more detail. *Cardinal rule 2: Variety is the spice of life* dives into a deeper explanation of putting together a plan that appeals to several customer segments. We'll look at what works and what doesn't so you'll spend money on the right items when it's time to take the plunge and purchase merchandise.

CARDINAL RULE 2: VARIETY IS THE SPICE OF LIFE

'**DO YOU CARRY *HETALIA?*' ASKS** one attendee. 'Do you carry *Fairy Tail*?' asks another. 'Do you have *League of Legends* key chains?' 'Ooh, please, please tell me you have *Pokémon* Charizard?'

What these questions tell you is that your customers have specific wants crossing several anime shows and video games. The previous cardinal rule made it Windex-clear that thoroughly knowing and understanding your customer and delivering what they want is the ultimate key to success. This rule expands on this so you can meet the needs of several customer segments with your merchandise.

Think about the last con you went to. What was it that the vendors all had in common? You got it. Almost every single vendor sold a variety of merchandise from multiple anime shows. And this brings us to *Cardinal rule 2: Variety is the spice of life.*

Only a few vendors will exclusively sell just one category of item. Sword (props) or T-shirt vendors are more likely to fall into this category. However, sword vendors, for example, will typically secure exclusivity from the convention so that they are the only game in town. The limited merchandise mix works well in this instance. But this is not so with vendors selling products from just one anime series or only one category of merchandise. When you select your merchandise, you want to appeal to several customer targets, not just one or two!

Recently, my booth was located across the aisle from a T-shirt vendor. The vendor's sales for the three-day convention were 'okay,' in his words. But throngs of attendees walked right past his booth. Why? Most of them weren't interested in his T-shirt designs – and that was all he had.

I've seen vendors selling only *Hello Kitty* plushies. Not everyone loves *Hello Kitty*, who fans recently learned is not a cat. She is a little girl. Her real name is Kitty White and she was born in southern England on November 1, 1974. She is a Scorpio and her blood type is A. But I digress...

Vendors who target only one customer segment such as chess players who like magic or *Hello Kitty* plushy lovers generally suffer a slow death at conventions. Their merchandise appeal is restricted to a narrow pool of people. And their customers, by the way, may be more interested in other stuff at the convention. To make matters worse, other vendors are also selling the same items in addition to other merchandise, which appeals to multiple customer segments and increases their foot traffic.

You might think that having a narrow focus will enable you to have more sizes and styles available, but attendees can often purchase the same type of merchandise from multiple vendors. The fact you have more sizes and styles will only be relevant to the few convention-goers who are fanatical about a particular size or style that is not available elsewhere. So don't go down this lonely, unprofitable path. Choose the path successful vendors travel.

Spice up your merchandise

A battle-tested merchandise plan appeals to several customer segments and caters to a variety of tastes. And these tastes vary across anime series and categories of merchandise. This tried and true course of action works because:

- You'll be competing more broadly against other vendors.
- More potential customers are attracted to your booth because you offer the variety they want.
- You have the opportunity to sell more products to each customer.
- Customers have a reason to visit your booth multiple times.
- Your risk is diversified – you don't bet everything on a few items.
- You can achieve more profit from higher sales.

Let's scrutinize a vendor example that has a good range of merchandise from a good range of anime (ahem, this vendor happens to be me) and then I'll explain why this works.

My vendor booth

My product mix includes six anime shows and ten different items from several merchandise categories:

- *Pokémon* plushies, key chains and hats
- *Dragon Ball Z* scouters and plushies
- Alpaca (llama) plushies
- *Attack on Titan* plushies, pillows and pocket watches
- *Black Butler* pocket watches, rings and necklaces
- *Full Metal Alchemist* pocket watches, figures and piggy banks
- A few other miscellaneous anime items

So, why these anime shows and items? Well, *Pokémon* is a wildly-popular, classic anime show. It is a cultural icon of Japan. And thanks to new video game releases, a steady stream of new characters, annual movie releases and a finely-tuned merchandising machine, fans are forever connected and searching for *Pokémon* merchandise.

Pokémon's list of characters exceeds 700 and grows daily. Every vendor carries at least a few of the most popular *Pokémon* plushies but no vendor can match my range. I stock approximately 150 of the legendary *Pokémon* as well as some unique *Pokémon* from later generations that are exclusively sold in Japan. The variety of plush characters at my booth appeals largely to the older fans who grew up on the earlier generations. This older customer segment is my primary *Pokémon* purchaser. On a side note, customers see my booth as it is pictured above and refer to me as the '*Pokémon* lady,' so you could say this is my primary focus.

Another favorite anime of con attendees is *Dragon Ball Z*. This show has been around for ages and was one of the first anime to broadcast on US television. The scouters, a prominent prop in the show, are one of my top-sellers, especially among the guys. Every fan knows Vegeta's famous line, 'It's over 9,000,' which I hear *three dozen* times a day. The scouters are cool, fun to wear and make great gifts for diehard fans. They're also a great way for a fan to get noticed in a sea of attendees because any fan wearing one is silently screaming, 'Look at me! Look at me!' Also, attendees LOVE taking selfies while wearing the scouters and then sharing those photos with friends.

Fans will also beat down the proverbial door to purchase alpacas. These little guys sprung to the top of the plushy must-have list seemingly out of nowhere. And while they weren't originally related to any particular anime, their adaptability to dress as characters from different shows has opened the door to unlimited varieties. I outsmart other vendors by being the first to find and stock the newest and 'cutest' creations.

Dr. Who Alpacas

Another good seller with long-term potential is my *Attack on Titan* merchandise. This show was a rare and explosive new series that gained massive popularity in both Japan and the US during its premier season. Much like *Pokémon*, every vendor has at least some *Attack on Titan* merchandise, mostly figures. So I focus on carrying other merchandise that is harder to obtain and exclusively distributed in Japan.

Black Butler is another popular anime that happens to be under-represented at conventions. There are fans at every con in elaborate *Black Butler* costumes, role-playing their favorite characters. This anime is not on other vendors' radar screens so at the request of many fans, I started carrying a wide selection of exclusive *Black Butler* merchandise.

You might be wondering how you can use my merchandise mix to develop your own merchandise plan. Well, there are several traits that mine and other successful vendor businesses share:

- First, my booth has an identity – the *Pokémon* booth.
- Second, it is easily-describable and, therefore, easy for attendees to find.
- Third, I sell both popular anime and popular merchandise categories.
- Fourth, I have an abundance of unique items on display.
- Finally, there is minimal overlap with other vendors.

Successful vendors target several customer segments by carrying a number of categories or items that are different, exclusive or have just been released on the market. But they also know when enough is enough.

Oops alert: At the last comic and sci-fi convention I attended, there was a vendor practicing the 'Walmart' philosophy. They had this mix: plushies and figures in every size known from several *dozen* anime and manga series. They also stocked backpacks, hats, posters, pocket watches, key chains, pillows, wall scrolls, cosplay outfits, necklaces, rings and more.

SELLING TO HEROES, VILLAINS AND GEEKS

> **!** Most of the *hundreds* of different items only appealed to a handful of, if any, fans. Sure, they got foot traffic and sales, but it was based mostly on the 80/20 rule. This is where eighty percent of the sales are generated from just twenty percent of the items. An important consideration here is that this vendor also needed four booth spaces to display everything, which came at a cost of $1,600. And by using the standard industry mark-up, I estimate they needed $3,200 in sales just to break even. Unfortunately, the convention was a ghost town for all three days and that vendor was definitely in the red by a few thousand dollars.

Why do some vendors pursue the 'Walmart' route? If I were to hazard a guess, it's because they hope to sell a ton of stuff of questionable quality that they have purchased at dirt-cheap prices. But being the 'Walmart' of anime vendors is a high-stakes game that you'll end up losing when other vendors carry more select, unique and exclusive merchandise. I notice a few of these 'Walmart' vendors roll their eyes when they see me at conventions. We're friendly but they know they'll lose plenty of business to me so they are not very enthusiastic, so I'm told, when they see me walk through the door. I'll keep this discussion PG so let's move right along.

Carrying an extensive product mix from such a large number of anime series impacts your business in two main ways:

- You have a bigger investment in inventory.
- You need multiple spaces at each convention.

Inventory will be your biggest investment so picking the right variety to appeal to your customer segments should be carefully thought through. And as the chart below demonstrates, your decision has financial repercussions throughout your business.

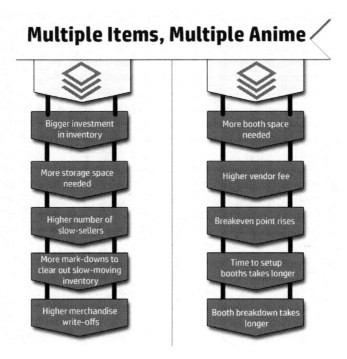

Variety is important so that your merchandise appeals to a large enough pool of targeted customers to enable you to be profitable. But too much variety leaves you in a financially-vulnerable position, not really appealing to anyone, and more likely to strike out with customers.

#JustTheRightSpice

When thinking about variety, you'll want to fine-tune your merchandise plan by narrowing the number of anime series and merchandise categories that you will stock. And then figure out the right combination. I'm sure you're thinking, 'How do I get from Point A (a large list of popular anime series and categories) to Point B (the right number of shows and the right items)?'

The best way is by focusing on unique or exclusive merchandise that is available from popular shows and discovering a niche for yourself. Up next, we'll study the wheel of unique merchandise. Working from the outside in, it shows various ways to arrive at the finish line.

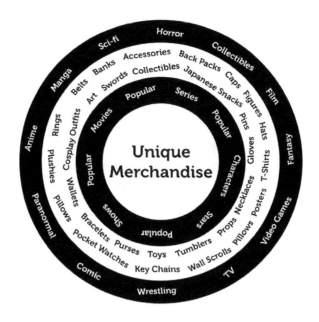

Wheel of Unique Merchandise

You can narrow down your merchandise options by beginning with a genre. You'll find a vast number of merchandise available for every show, movie, game, publication, edition or premier event. The 'Walmart' vendors end their search process here by stocking something from every possible combination. Your search, however, is just beginning. Within a genre, you want to weed out the lesser known shows and focus on ones that are still generating a ton of buzz with a large following. Notice, I didn't say start with what you already have in mind to sell. If you love a genre, start there. But let fans dictate where you go from here based on what's popular. Next, you'll gear up for numerous 'Google searches' to find unique merchandise that will set you apart from the crowd.

In the second part of this book, I'll explain the process of how to get hold of unique items. But for now, let's focus on another example of what a good merchandising mix looks like so you know what you're shooting for. The next example shows a vendor that has found a profitable unique niche, with a targeted customer segment, and spicy merchandise.

Horrorautographs.com's merchandise is truly inspired. It revolves around a unique idea with built-in exclusivity. The merchandise mix is the stuff that nightmares are made of – autograph memorabilia from the horror and thriller genres.

They sell pictures, original artwork, prints and props signed by the actors who played immortal or bloodthirsty murderers. This really speaks to the hearts of horror fans. Many movie psychos are represented, from Jason Voorhees (*Friday the 13th*), Michael Meyers (*Halloween*), Freddy Krueger (*Nightmare on Elm Street*), Pinhead (*Hellraiser*), Jigsaw (*Saw*), Leatherface (*Texas Chainsaw Massacre*) to The Walking Dead stars.

Freddy Krueger; Nightmare on Elm Street
Robert Englund signed original painting $299

Friday the 13th
Ari Lehman signed hockey mask $59

Jason Vorhees
Friday The 13th
Ari Lehman signed 11"x17" poster $49

The owner strays slightly from the core horror concept to appeal to a larger fan base by also selling Marvel photos and prints (such as *Spiderman, Hulk, Iron Man, The Avengers* and *Thor*) signed by Stan Lee. Pretty cool, huh? This is yet another reminder that it's of supreme importance to offer items of current popular shows or movies as well as your more niche items so that you attract more customers.

A merchandise plan like the one in this example does involve higher risk since the convention prices are outside the budget of most attendees. Also, his unusual merchandise, such as the machetes, moves at a much slower pace than standard convention items. But this plan can still generate several thousand dollars per convention.

Referring back to the wheel of unique merchandise, you'll notice the owner narrowed his focus to mainly one genre (horror), the most popular shows within the genre, and stocked unique and popular categories of merchandise (autographed prints and memorabilia) associated with that genre.

Did you figure out that the same traits that give my booth an edge over other vendors are in play with this example too? Horrorautographs.com has a clear identity, their booth is easily-describable, they sell popular anime and merchandise categories, they have an abundance of unique items on display, and they have minimal overlap with other vendors. If you follow all of the cardinal rules, you'll see these successful traits naturally emerge with your booth without any extra work required on your part.

So, while variety is definitely the spice of life (and cons!), what you don't want to do is try to stock every piece of merchandise from every anime series ever made. Impossible! What you want to do – no, *must* do – is get a variety of unique merchandise from a manageable number of popular anime series so that you appeal to several customer targets. This may not seem like an earth-shattering revelation, but all too often new vendors kill their business prospects before they even start because they don't sell the merchandise customers want to buy. If you get this wrong, it's over. End of story.

In our next cardinal rule, you'll discover how to identify, search and source the unique and exclusive merchandise you need to set you apart. My goal is to steadily arm you with the means to wage a fierce fight for the convention-goer's dollars – and win!

CARDINAL RULE 3: THINK DIFFERENT

'**AAAIIIIEEEEE! I'VE BEEN LOOKING EVERYWHERE** for this,' she blurts out. 'Wow. I can't believe I found this,' he says. 'Wait, I've never seen this before!'

You know you're getting it right when your booth is the epicenter of these screams. And this brings us to *Cardinal rule 3: Think different*.

Convention-goers literally scream with delight or gasp for breath when they come across a vendor selling must-have-or-I'll-die merchandise. I've had to calm customers down by telling them to take several deep breaths. Thankfully, I've never needed to perform CPR, but a few stampeding fans have knocked over my displays trying to be the first to grab an item. Fans get so excited about unique merchandise that their hands literally shake as they dig through their backpacks searching for the money to buy it.

To get fans super excited about your merchandise, you need to stock your booth with exclusive anime or manga items that other vendors don't carry. Exclusive merchandise doesn't necessarily mean one-of-a-kind items. What it means is that there is some kind of product difference between what you have and what is commonly available. This difference might be quite minor, for example, an item related to a secondary character (not the main one), or it can be a significant departure from standard convention merchandise, for example, a ninja sword umbrella.

Dare to be different

Don't be a clone. When numerous vendors sell the same popular items, attendees will go from booth to booth in search of the cheapest price. To distinguish your merchandise from other vendors and avoid competing only on price, take the road less traveled to find exclusive, unique or hard-to-obtain popular items. You're new to the business. As a new vendorpreneur, you want to distinguish yourself from the start or the competition will squash you.

So, where do you start? What will make your booth special? Why should anyone pause at your booth instead of the hundreds of others? Why should attendees purchase anything from you? What can you stock that other vendors don't? We'll start by digging to the core of several merchandise strategies and seeing which ones you can adopt to differentiate your merchandise from what other vendors sell. Heads up! The following strategies aren't mutually exclusive and the most profitable plan will include all three.

Strategy 1: Minor product difference

You can carry almost the exact same merchandise as the vendor next to you, yet be seen as different and sell ten times more. How? By sourcing an item that is commonly available but has a minor variation in the color, pose, size, design, character or material.

Identifying the variation that will have the highest customer appeal for each item requires more time than most vendors want to invest. But if you are prepared to do a little research, it can pay big dividends. A different pose, design or larger size can have a surprising impact on sales and give you a big advantage over other vendors with similar items.

When I am searching for popular items with minor product differences, I try to avoid the common styles offered by the major suppliers. I seek out distributors that offer a twist in design, color or size so that I have something unique to offer fans. When I react to a picture of an item with, 'Ooh, that's really cute,' or, 'Wow, I haven't seen that before,' I know I'm onto a winner.

For example, consider the Japanese arpakasso amuse alpacasso, otherwise referred to as alpacas, which are currently a hot-seller. I noticed these alpacas selling briskly at another vendor's booth and decided to look into them for my booth. (As a vendor you always need to keep your eyes open for new ideas.) While I was searching for an alpaca supplier, I uncovered a tidbit about buyer preference. Apparently the alpacas with little hats perched on their heads were the most popular style internationally.

However, most suppliers were selling alpacas with a scarf around their neck (as opposed to the little hats) and, therefore, most vendors were stocking this style. The scarf style was cute but the alpacas with the hats were *really* cute. It took a bit more effort to source these, but it was worth it because a large number of attendees preferred this style. I was competing head-to-head with other vendors, but this minor product difference gave me the advantage and I enjoyed more sales.

Alpacas (38cm x 28cm)

This is just one example; I've found other product variations can evoke different emotions and lead to a purchase too. Minor tweaks that can add a bounce to your sales include:

- Color (light blue-green or pink are very popular).
- Size (some items as tiny as 3 inches tug at the heart of customers, or items offered in a bigger size, like 12 inches, are also prone to be snatched up).
- Pose (sitting versus standing or sleeping versus awake).
- Material (that's Charmin® soft to the touch).
- And I hate to sound sexist but speaking to my male readers, if your cute-o-meter is not working – ask a female friend. I'm serious. Cute items sell and *really* cute items sell better. Do your homework on which product variations customers emotionally overreact to and reap the rewards. In many instances, a minor tweak will make a noticeable sales difference.

Strategy 2: Medium product difference

A medium product difference involves sourcing an item that is popular but has something special about it that makes it unique. It might have a special feature, limited quantity produced, or its availability in the US is sparse.

For example, pocket watches are a favorite con item and they range in price from $15 to $35. The problem is that most vendors are in direct competition with each other, offering the exact same watch from the same popular anime. I mentioned earlier that *Black Butler* is one of the anime on sale at my booth. To separate my *Black Butler* pocket watches from others, I source higher-quality watches that are only distributed in Japan and rarely make their way to US vendors or buyers.

Black Butler 'Book of Circus' Joker pocket watch

By doing this, I'm still selling *Black Butler* pocket watches like other vendors but there is a significant difference in appearance, quality and availability. Attendees stop to admire the Japanese watches with the black clock face, color silhouette and heavy frame. They appreciate the quality and soon realize that they're only available at my booth. *Black Butler* fans happily pay the $35 price because it is appropriate given the exclusivity and uniqueness.

Another good example of items with a medium product difference is limited edition figures of popular characters. Currently, Funko Pop! is the brand of figures *du jour* and practically every single figure vendor has rows and rows of them. They are priced at $10 to $12 with no room for price mobility because the exact same figure is available at dozens of booths. So a better competitive strategy is to source limited edition figures from high-end toy companies (such as, Revoltech, Sculpture Arts, Square Enix, Play Arts, Good Smile Company, Banpresto, Bandai or DC Comics).

Figure vendors going the high-end route can charge eighty dollars and upwards, with prices regularly exceeding a hundred dollars. Competition is less fierce and there are more exclusive or unique figures available compared to the Funko Pop! figures.

Funko Pop! Figure $10   *DC Comics $125*

If you can source popular items that have a medium product difference, you'll do a better job of piquing fans' interest than vendors who stock the standard stuff that everyone has.

Strategy 3: Major product difference

A major product difference involves stocking items that make customers glance and then do a double-take when walking past your booth. The items are surprising or unexpected among the range of available merchandise displayed at every other booth.

Standing apart from the vendor pack can pay big dividends if you get it right. We looked at horrorautographs.com in the previous cardinal rule and they've mastered the major product difference strategy. But carrying a line of merchandise that is not from any of the major categories can be a risky proposition. New vendors frequently venture into areas not relevant or attractive to attendees. Remember the chess set and magic card vendor we talked about earlier?

Other vendors have tried their hand at steampunk (a subgenre of science fiction) and chainmail merchandise to try and carve out a niche for their business. Steampunk focuses on items made from gears, sprockets, clock hands and watch parts, and chainmail is a type of armor with small metal rings linked together in a pattern. Their pool of potential buyers is miniscule or may not even exist for most of their merchandise. That's not to say that you *can't* succeed with this strategy. These booths do attract customers, but nowhere near the foot traffic or sales of the vendors selling more traditional con items.

A great example of a major product difference that worked at a recent anime and comic convention was socks. Yes, socks were a hot-seller. Who knew?! In your wildest dreams, could you imagine anyone jumping up and down with joy because they found socks? Nah, I couldn't have imagined it either. But the vendor in question certainly caught the attention of convention-goers. They sold *Superman*, *Batman* and *Spiderman* crew socks along with socks emblazoned with skulls, cats, skeletons, footballs and animals. They sold the boutique brands K. Bell, SockSmith and hypnyc, whose fun, fashionable footwear turned out to be surprisingly popular.

Sock display at comic convention

Since they were my booth neighbor, I observed the reactions of convention-goers. I noticed a whole list of interesting facts. First, this was the only time I had ever seen a sock retailer at a convention. Second, the booth drew a lot of foot traffic (no pun intended). Third, 'You need socks' was a common statement coming from the women to their children or partner. Fourth, prices were reasonable at about $7–9 a pair. Fifth, this out-of-the-box event for a sock retailer guaranteed vendor exclusivity (and will continue to do so until word gets out to other sock retailers). And finally, most customers purchased three to six pairs. The vendor sold in excess of 300 pairs over the weekend! And this was their very first pop culture event.

So, products with a major difference can prove to be popular items even though they are significantly different from the usual anime merchandise. But be mindful that a lot of new-to-the-convention-scene merchandise often proves to be a bust. You want to keep cardinal rules 1 and 2 in mind when you stray off the path of the more commonly-sought-after merchandise.

All in all, combining all three of these strategies gives you the best chance of success with the least risk. Veteran convention customers are smart. They check the price of generic-looking items at several different vendors, *as well* as on Amazon and eBay with their smartphone, before they make a purchase. You don't want to be forced to compete on price alone. Stocking exclusive or unique items means there is no price comparison and often no competition.

Unearthing unique items in a different country

The next challenge, of course, is actually finding unique and exclusive items that you want to stock. One way to do this is to source merchandise directly from Japan. Con attendees LOVE authentic Japanese anime and manga items and are willing to pay a higher price.

The anime, manga and gaming companies continually release new items that are sold only in Japan. These merchandise releases are for a limited time only and in limited quantities. Because the distribution is limited to Japan, US fans do not have easy and affordable access. This makes the merchandise highly sought-after when they're sold at conventions. As a vendor, you want to tap into the Japanese distribution channel to purchase these items. Let's begin by examining one of the main and fascinating sales channels that Japanese companies use to get merchandise into the hands of their fans.

Licensed distributors such as Nintendo, Game Freak, Banpresto, Bandai, SEGA and Takara Tomy release a vast range of high-quality anime merchandise via arcade games. Yes, arcade games! Anything and everything imaginable is available. Think: plushies, figures, plates, banks, pocket watches, key chains, video games, food, posters, blankets, swords, and the list goes on. Sizes range from small to super big and values range from inexpensive to expensive.

Japan arcade 'claw' game; win a sword

Another way that Japanese fans can get merchandise is through the 'Ichiban kuji' (lottery), where they can win items. The lottery items are as varied and numerous as the arcade prizes. Fans purchase tickets sold all over Japan in convenience stores or bookshops. Every ticket purchaser wins a prize. These prizes are not for sale, so if a fan misses out in the lottery, the only way to acquire them is to buy them through online auction sites afterwards. Therefore, the prizes become very valuable.

Prizes won at the arcade or through Ichiban kuji are immediately sold online. They go straight from the arcade to a Japanese eBay-like auction site and there are hundreds of thousands of items available from every anime, manga and video game in every category of merchandise on the planet.

The most popular site is Yahoo auction (auctions.yahoo.co.jp). It functions just like eBay, except it's in Japanese. Rakuten auction (auction.rakuten.co.jp) and Amazon Japan (amazon.co.jp) are other well-known sites where you can purchase unique or exclusive merchandise. The items offered for sale are brand new, unopened goods in the original package. We won't get into the nuts and bolts of the purchasing process at this stage, but it's a good time to sample the Japanese prizes that become hot property at US cons.

The next few pages present pictures of a *miniscule* array of arcade and lottery prizes.

Pokémon Pikachu Face Cushion (lottery prize)

Pokémon Pikachu with Japanese Soccer uniform (arcade game)

Pokémon Pikachu Pokéball (lottery prize)

Fullmetal Alchemist Piggy Bank (lottery prize)

Fullmetal Alchemist Alphonse Plush (arcade game)

Hello Kitty Plush (arcade game)

Hello Kitty Plush (arcade game)

Black Butler Pocket Watches (arcade game)

Black Butler Sebastian and Ciel figures (arcade game)

Attack on Titan figure (arcade game)

Attack on Titan pocket watches (arcade game)

SELLING TO HEROES, VILLAINS AND GEEKS

Thanks to the unending stream of unique or exclusive merchandise flowing through arcade games and lottery promotions – not to mention the merchandise released through normal Japanese retail channels – there are ample purchasing opportunities for unique stock. It's a matter of knowing where to look and putting in the effort to acquire it. Plan to allocate a large portion of your time searching for products that will populate your merchandise plan.

> There are assignments and step-by-step instructions on how to search for sought-after Japanese items and purchase them in *Part 2: Business battle plan blueprint*.

Furry Hats

Outside of Japan, a second resource you can use to find unique or exclusive items is the Chinese website taobao.com. This shopping retail site offers an Amazon-like menu of items in multiple categories – clothing, electronics, home furnishings, sporting equipment, toys, and so on. If you spend time searching this site, you can stumble across new items that are unique to the convention scene. I came across this website purely by accident when looking for alpaca suppliers. What I found, besides alpacas, were these furry hats that were Charmin® soft.

I had occasionally seen attendees sporting these type of hats at cons, so when I saw the ridiculously-low price for them on this site, I decided to purchase them (forgetting all about the alpacas). I selected the styles that offered a medium product difference for my inventory. I charged between $25 and $30 for these and they SOLD OUT on the first day at the very first convention I put them on display.

> You'll find more information on the Chinese purchasing process in *Part 2: Business battle plan blueprint*.

As a new vendor, it is imperative that you burst through the throngs of vendor booths and grab convention-goers' attention with merchandise that stops them in their tracks.

You're probably experiencing mental fatigue as you try to juggle all three of the cardinal rules we have discussed so far. But profitable vendors do it all the time when they investigate and select merchandise to stock. Remember, you're learning how to give customers what they want, how to spice up your merchandise with a range of items from a range of anime, and how to be unique with your offerings. But the rules don't end here. We have two more to go.

Once you locate unique or exclusive merchandise, you must determine the convention price for each of the items. Pricing is tricky and new vendors are guessing in the dark, typically overpricing, which spawns the fourth do-or-die cardinal rule: *Avoid customer price shock*.

CARDINAL RULE 4: AVOID CUSTOMER PRICE SHOCK

'I'LL TAKE IT.' 'HOW MUCH? I'll buy it!' 'Ooh, it's only $20, I gotta have it.' 'I've been looking for this, and it's only $15.' Versus this: 'What? It's $45! There is no f***ing way I'm paying that!'

Setting the right price on your merchandise is eighty-five percent science, ten percent situation, five percent art and zero percent greed. Being outrageous with your prices gets you nowhere. Attendees are not idiots; they know when a vendor's aggressive prices are a rip-off. Yes, you're in the business to turn a profit, but customer faces should never register sticker shock when viewing your prices. And that is what *Cardinal rule 4: Avoid customer price shock* is all about.

Every customer allocates their money across the con registration fee, celebrity photo-ops, autographs, food, parking and extra events (such as maid café or dance) *as well* as their dealer-room purchases. So grabbing a sizeable share of each fan's limited budget needs to top your priority list. Other vendors and artists are competing for this same pool of dollars and if they are selling merchandise for noticeably-lower and more reasonable prices than you, you'll attract window shoppers but not paying customers. And, consequently, you'll fall well short of your sales goal.

I remember making a killing at one large convention because other plushy vendors must have been smokin' something when they set their prices. Attendees kept returning to my booth complaining about the other vendors' super high prices. For instance, they were selling one plushy for $35 that normally sells for $20. Remember, veteran con-goers will check all of the vendor prices before making a purchase, and they don't take kindly to vendors who try to rip off unsuspecting attendees.

Attendees will quickly fall out of love with an item at a vendor's booth if the price is way out of line with what is reasonable. Luckily for them, at conventions there is always something new to love right down the aisle – like at my booth. I sold enough stuff at that particular convention for it to place in my top three bestselling conventions of the year. Sometimes other vendors and their crazy prices are *my* best sales tool.

Pricing best practices

Vendors often forget they're not the only game in town when they set their prices. It's important to remember that convention-goers check all vendor prices before making a purchase. And the more diligent ones will also check Amazon and eBay. So you have to regularly investigate what the competition is charging and price your merchandise accordingly. In *Part 2*, we'll look at examples of assigning prices to items to generate the most profit. But, for now, consider the following points as you develop your own pricing strategy:

- Your prices should reflect the value of your item compared to the competition. If pocket watches sell between $15 and $35, then charging $80 is out of line and severely shrinks the number of potential buyers.

- Your prices should match what attendees will actually pay. If *everyone* shakes their head and walks away, then your prices are clearly exceeding the value customers assign to your items.

- Price your items in whole dollars only and don't add cents like $0.49 or $0.99. This is standard vendor practice for anime merchandise (excluding Japanese snacks).

- Your prices should enable you to reach your convention sales goal. The trap here is when convention attendance falls well below the con's projection. A convention may expect 2,000 people but maybe only 600 attend. Ratchet your sales goal up or down based on convention turn out and cross the con off your list for next year if it's a dud.

- Your prices should cover your expenses. Calculate how much profit you need to generate to cover your investment, including the convention cost and other business expenses.

- Your prices should maximize your profits. Setting prices too low means you are passing up profit that could be yours to enjoy. If you can sell an item for a higher price, go for it. I once sold *Attack on Titan* pillows for $15 and they constantly sold out. So, I started charging $18 and continued to achieve the same sales result. However, when I tried $20, sales slowed significantly so I reverted back to $18, which proved the most profitable price in this case.

Attack on Titan pillows

These pricing guidelines are a great starting point. But you also need to understand that price is not just a dollar amount. It's a quality cue. It subtly communicates many things about your merchandise. It influences customer behavior and their willingness to buy or otherwise pass on an item.

The psychology of pricing

There is an infinite amount of research that analyzes the psychological component of pricing on customer behavior littering corporate market research departments. So, what do these reports conclude about pricing?

As a general principle, a higher price translates to a higher perceived value in the customer's mind.

Price	=	**Perceived value**
High price	=	High value, high quality
Low price	=	Low value, low quality

This means that a higher price suggests that the quality simply must be there.

But let's be crystal clear, you can't slap a high price on any old item and expect your customers to just pay it. The item has to have some visual cue or inherent value that supports the high price. As a vendor, there are a couple of ways to increase the perceived value on an item so you can price *and sell* a plushy for $35 without seeming unreasonable.

One way is to limit the quantity available. Research suggests that the psychological impact of scarce supply causes an increase in demand from customers. This happens with the merchandise in Japan where entertainment companies produce and release limited quantities and sell them for a limited period of time.

A US example is Hasbro, which executes this principle masterfully at conventions. At San Diego Comic-Con, Hasbro's sales line for its limited-edition toys reaches capacity just *ten minutes* after opening. Attendees are desperate to get the toys before the words 'SOLD OUT' are said over and over again by the Hasbro representative. Without a doubt, Hasbro intentionally restricts supply as a strategy to create demand for its high-priced toys. Also, scarcity goes hand-in-hand with uniqueness and both play equal parts in shaping an item's perceived value.

In an extreme example, a pristine copy of *Action Comics No. 1* (the comic book that introduced the Man of Steel to the world in 1938) sold for $3,207,852 on eBay! Both the scarcity and uniqueness contributed to this item's extraordinarily-high perceived value. You probably should stock items just a little bit less unique than this at your booth though.

Another way to increase perceived value and positively impact customer behavior centers on the lowest and highest price points you set for a group of items. When you're offering more than one product in the same category of items, their relative prices can greatly distort the perceived value of each individual product. So, price *a few* items in the category slightly above their maximum perceived value. This is called price anchoring *and* gives your customers a frame of reference when valuing your items.

This can enable you to guide your customers towards choosing the exact product you want them to choose at the exact price you want them to buy it – almost like a Jedi mind trick. For instance, I originally sold *Pokémon* plushies at these price points: $5, $10, $20 and $30. The $30 plushies were slow-sellers until I added a few higher-priced plushies for $40. Before I could blink, the sales of my $30 plushies, which were more profitable for me, doubled without diminishing my sales at the lower price points. The $30 plushies were no longer my highest priced items and seemed, in the customer's mind, a much better deal than the $40 plushies. And, if I sold a few $40 plushies, which I would have normally priced at $30, my profit pool increases more because I effectively used price anchoring.

Customers are making price comparisons all the time. You can take control of those comparisons by positioning your most profitable items next to something more expensive. Customers will automatically perceive your lower-priced items as more affordable. If you don't, your customers will probably find comparisons of their own by visiting other vendors, and you may end up losing sales.

So another advantage of stocking unique and exclusive merchandise is that you can charge a higher price than you would for commonly-available items and customers can't compare prices at other vendors because they don't carry these items. But you have to strike the right price balance so your sales volume remains high.

How high is too high?

A higher price typically means lower volume. If attendees are extremely sensitive to an item's price, you're better off setting a much lower price and selling a considerably-higher volume. Yet, in some cases, you may generate more total profit with fewer sales at the higher price.

If you charge $5 or $10 above your current price and sales barely decline, you'll make more profit. It all depends on the item's perceived value and if there are competitive alternatives. Be flexible. You might need to rethink your pricing once you see how other vendors are pricing their stuff that day.

If you offer a truly-unique product with little competition, it can be challenging to set the right price. You will need to conduct a market test to make sure your prices are optimized to generate the most profit possible. You can do this by testing different prices on the same item at a few different conventions.

Track which price generated the best sales volume for the item and then check which strategy gave you the best overall profit. Was it the lower price and higher volume? Or the higher price and lower volume?

To negotiate or not to negotiate?

You'll definitely get attendees who want to negotiate a cheaper price or make a special deal with you. Some of them think they're at a flea market! Whether or not you decide to give customers wiggle room on the price, you should be consistent and maintain that position throughout the weekend.

My stance on negotiating is this: I don't. Period. I politely and apologetically decline any offers for a lower price. I've lost less than a dozen customers out of the thousands who went on to buy even when I wouldn't entertain the idea of a 30% discount. Let's analyze this stance by assuming you're at a convention and standing in your booth.

A customer walks up to you and offers to pay $10 less than the posted price. If you negotiate with them, you will have to negotiate with everyone standing at your booth who is listening in at that moment. And who wants to do that all weekend? Vendor booths can get very busy and if customers within earshot hear you giving a discount to one person, they'll want a discount too (even if they would have happily paid your advertised price otherwise). No, thank you.

 Sensei tip: Customers repeatedly say they don't have enough money for a particular item. But don't be quick to offer a lower price. They always, somehow, out of the blue, find more money. Many times, they open a wallet bulging with a stack of bills and hand you $100. After you experience this a few times, you'll be cured of the temptation to offer a discounted price.

Some vendors, however, willingly offer a discount to every customer who shows the slightest interest in an item. There is nothing wrong with this. But if offering discounts is a part of your sales strategy then you need to make sure you build this into your prices. A lot more thought goes into pricing than you probably anticipated. As long as you avoid the extremes – too high or too low – you'll do fine at your first few conventions. Other vendor prices of comparable items are a good benchmark if you're unsure about the right price for an item. Ultimately, though, your prices need to reflect the quality and uniqueness of your merchandise. The more appealing your merchandise is, the more customers are willing to pay.

Hang in there; we have one more cardinal rule to cover before we really get down to your personal business plan. We have built the foundations relevant to this in the first four rules, yet this next rule bears a separate focus. A boatload of work goes into executing *Cardinal rule 5: Ferocious bargain hunter* correctly.

CARDINAL RULE 5: FEROCIOUS BARGAIN HUNTER

BLACK FRIDAY SALES DRIVE NORMALLY-SANE people insane as they search for the best advertised bargains. Stuff we would never buy at its regular price becomes such a good bargain that we just can't resist. Many customers line up at unheard-of hours just to be the first in line to buy. Everybody likes a good bargain and vendors are no exception.

This leads right to *Cardinal rule 5: Ferocious bargain hunter*. Acquiring merchandise at the lowest price possible and then selling it at the highest price possible means long term success for any business. Simply stated, you must 'buy low, sell high.'

Unfortunately, the vendor's version of the Black Friday sales doesn't happen very often. Sure, you can stumble across great bargains from time to time, but your regular suppliers are going to be your primary source for your merchandise. And they're also practicing this rule.

Your suppliers can include other retailers, wholesalers and individuals with small online businesses located either here or abroad. Even eBay, yes, eBay, can be a source of merchandise for your business. At any point in time, any one of these options might be offering a better price on certain items than your normal source. There's no sugar coating this – searching online for the absolute lowest price consumes a massive amount of time. Searching for the best purchase price and the right auction or supplier can span three hours, three days, three weeks or three months.

Prowling for bargain prices

Whether you are searching for American or international suppliers, you need to constantly pursue the lowest possible price before every major purchase you make. Let's start by looking at American suppliers.

American suppliers

According to my comic vendor friends, Diamond Comic Distributors is the world's largest distributor of English-language comics, graphic novels and pop-culture-related merchandise. However, only businesses with a brick and mortar store can open a wholesale account with them, which may prevent you from accessing their wholesale prices. Numerous other American wholesale options exist but their requirements for opening a business account may also be outside of your reach. A solution to challenges like this can be partnering with other vendors or storeowners. The partnership accomplishes two things: Your combined orders will meet some hefty minimum purchase requirements and you'll be able to give a physical retail location on the wholesale account application form.

Of course, there are non-wholesaler options you can use that include numerous online retailers who offer exclusive items with discounts. You can score big wins by scouring these sites for the best possible prices. I've stumbled across some excellent deals and some crazy new items while conducting price searches on American websites. I've also hit roadblocks when the pre-orders sold out, some great discounts had recently expired or out-of-stock notices were prevalent on numerous sale items.

Persistence is your best weapon. Be persistent and don't stop searching until you find what you're looking for. For example, I've gone from one American supplier to the next to purchase *Dragon Ball Z* scouters at a deep discount. The retailers only had limited quantities and my orders cleaned them out. But I always keep my eyes open for these or other items that are available at a great price right here at home.

Sensei tip: Sign up for email alerts and newsletters from retailers even if you don't purchase merchandise from them. You'll be immediately notified of upcoming product releases or sales. You never know what will catch your eye and you can search other retailers for a better price.

International suppliers

What you sell ultimately decides where you'll source supply. And since *Selling to Heroes, Villains and Geeks* focuses on unique anime items, your source is likely to be overseas. Both Japan and China are major suppliers of anime merchandise.

Prowling for bargains in Japan

We have already learned that Japan is the hotbed of unique anime merchandise. The arcade and Ichiban kuji distributors are officially licensed to create and sell a range of trademarked merchandise within their country. But there's no way for small vendors to access these distributors or trademark owners' wholesale prices but purchasing items at retail prices is widely accessible.

> We'll learn how to purchase items at inexpensive retail prices in *Part 2: Business battle plan blueprint.*

Even though Japan is several thousand miles way, it is fertile ground for bargains due to several factors. First, the items are priced cheap compared to American retail prices. Second, there are two unusual and inexpensive sales channels used for distribution. Third, there is a very favorable currency exchange rate. And lastly, there is an abundant supply of merchandise from every anime, whether it is new, old, ancient or in the future. Even though each individual item may have limited quantities produced, the large number of items overall gives anime fans the upper hand in the supply and demand equation. Distributors are forced to keep their prices low because the fans have almost unlimited choices.

While you'll incur other costs as a part of the overseas acquisition process, scores of good deals can be found in Japan, making it a worthwhile option. Ugh, this sounds like a lot of work, doesn't it? And it is. But what makes these deals worth pursuing is the high price you'll be able to charge for these items in the US. Convention fans are interested in authentic Japanese merchandise and they're willing to pay a premium price to add them to their collection. However, not all vendors take this authentic route and instead prefer to find non-authentic bargains from Chinese wholesalers.

Prowling for bargains in China

We've all heard about the Gucci handbags sold on the streets of Manhattan for $30. Yes, we know they're fakes but there's no need to kiss and tell. Which brings us to a heated debate about the pirated or bootleg merchandise from China sold at conventions.

All shows 'technically' prohibit bootleg items. Still, the enforcement of this tends to be either a full frontal assault or nonexistent. Conventions that have a laundry list of prohibited items and threaten to banish offenders to another planet are serious about bootleg merchandise. However, others that devote only three or four sentences to this in the vendor application will not be hiring any bootleg police. Veteran vendors invariably know which conventions are strict on bootleg items and which don't care. And until you do, caution is advised. But there are other considerations to be aware of in the 'legitimate versus bootleg item' debate too.

The anime and manga industry's estimated worth tops a billion dollars. But as with any large entertainment business, piracy of copyright material is rampant and affects the sales of legitimate merchandise. As a result, the industry has not shown any growth for several years and plenty of fans are bemoaning this stagnation in their blog posts. So both conventions and fan bloggers urge people to show their beloved industry support by purchasing merchandise from vendors who stock items from licensed distributors.

The other side of this debate is quite simple, though. Bootleg items are super cheap, plentiful, mostly good quality, easily acquired and fit nicely within most fans' budgets. The side of the fence vendors ultimately land on is heavily influenced by sales, profit margins and the amount of effort they want to expend finding unique items at bargain prices. For new vendors, you must avoid the easy (but risky) route of relying on Chinese wholesalers as your sole source of supply. I guarantee that you will be competing head-to-head with other vendors who are more experienced at doing this. Also, customers will be more attracted to your booth because of your unique merchandise and not the knock-offs that plenty of other vendors will be selling.

Sensei tip: You need to be aware of legitimate items that are knocked off by Chinese manufacturers, particularly if you are stocking the legitimate version. You'll have to avoid having too large of a price gap between the legitimate item and the bootleg version. There are plenty of customers who will pay the higher price as long as the difference doesn't cause their heart to stop.

> **Oops alert:** Right at the beginning of a large convention, a US licensed distributor for several Japanese anime properties walked around the dealer room handing out cease and desist letters to vendors selling bootleg merchandise that infringed on their copyright license. This killed the sales of one vendor, who had purchased four booth spaces ($3,200) and only sold bootleg merchandise.

As a vendor, you'll need to make some decisions about what merchandise you will stock and what your stance is on authenticity.

Avoiding supplier hiccups

Of course, whether you get your merchandise from the US or from international suppliers, there will always be hiccups you will have to deal with. Here are a few of my top tips to help minimize disruption in your purchasing and restocking timeline:

- Make sure you have several suppliers. There are times when one or more of your preferred suppliers will be out of stock or only have a small quantity of what you want available. Finding a new supplier at the last moment is not ideal because it can extend the time it takes to restock your inventory.

- There will be times when suppliers move slower than normal when shipping your order, so don't cut it too close when you need to receive new inventory. If you're in a rush to receive your next shipment, send the supplier an email explaining the date you need the shipment to arrive by. However, don't pay exorbitant shipping costs. The email alone usually helps to move your order to the top of the supplier's fulfillment queue. Inevitably, though, there will be instances when your bestselling items just won't arrive in time for your next convention. We've all been there; just do your best to avoid this.

- Avoid placing orders around holidays when businesses are closed. It's best to place a big order prior to a major holiday period if you need to restock for a convention that'll happen shortly after the holidays. For example, orders placed during the Thanksgiving and Christmas period always take longer to arrive. So order inventory for January conventions by the end of October at the latest.

- Like the US, Japan and China also celebrate holidays that you'll need to be aware of. For example, all businesses in China close for three and a half consecutive weeks sometime between January and March to celebrate the Chinese New Year. Plan accordingly.

- On rare occasions, international shipments delivered by the United States Postal Service can get stuck in customs for weeks in either ISC Chicago or ISC New York (ISC stands for International Service Center). Erase any thought about trying to get information on what's going on. Don't call; you'll get a recorded message. And don't stress. 'What will be, will be' is the only attitude worth taking here because you ain't going to get any information from USPS.

Whether you source your merchandise from the US, Japan or China, you need to keep in mind the battle cry: 'Buy low, sell high!' Vending is a business, so you want to make money on your merchandise. If you can purchase your stock for great prices, you can price them reasonably so they are more attractive to customers. And the cheaper you buy them, the more profit there'll be for you.

CARDINAL RULES WRAP-UP

What we've covered so far may not be brain surgery or rocket science but succeeding in the vendor business requires as much work and learning as any other profession. These five rules are truths. They work no matter who practices them. Unfortunately, many new vendors jump in without really understanding the business and how to proceed.

Stay out of trouble and place your business squarely in the profitable camp by adhering to the five cardinal rules:

- **Cardinal rule 1: Customer Con**
  The customer is boss. Your booth should feature items from anime and manga that customers want to buy. Following this rule is your prime directive.

- **Cardinal rule 2: Variety is the spice of life**
  Carry items from several different anime and merchandise categories. Not only do your customers have a variety of tastes, you want your merchandise to be sought after by several customer segments.

- **Cardinal rule 3: Think different**
  Unique or exclusive items not carried by other vendors can be the juggernaut behind your merchandise plan. Customers will be fascinated by your booth and falling over each other to purchase your items.

- **Cardinal rule 4: Avoid customer price shock**
  Your prices should reflect the value of the item and be comparable to what other vendors are charging for similar

merchandise. The more unique or exclusive the item, the higher the perceived value and you can charge a higher price.

- **Cardinal rule 5: Ferocious bargain hunter**
  Scour the Internet for the lowest-possible purchase price. Suppliers both here and overseas should regularly be investigated to secure your merchandise at a bargain price.

Wow, those were some jam-packed rules! It's time to put pen to paper and hash out your business battle plan. You are now going to practice what I've been preaching. There is nothing better than working through the situations you'll frequently face in order to hammer home the value of each rule. You'll find step-by-step instructions to put your business on the right path. Don't relax just yet – building and implementing your business battle plan demands hard work. Try to embrace the planning process; it will make a huge difference to the success of your new business.

PART 2:

BUSINESS BATTLE PLAN BLUEPRINT

Congratulations on making it to this point! When you operate with knowledge, you sabotage any chance of failure. And that knowledge is most powerful when it is formulated into a well-thought-out plan of action. The power to accomplish whatever you want burns within you.

In this part of the book, you'll be narrowing your focus to the hottest and most popular merchandise. You'll research the latest news and information on the top anime series to point you in the right direction, both online and based on what you see with your own eyes at conventions. You'll practice finding and selecting unique or exclusive merchandise and then acquiring it at the lowest price so that you bank the most profit. You'll practice sourcing merchandise, navigating the purchasing process, setting your convention prices and, ultimately, you will build your business battle plan.

You'll be guided through each step and will complete interactive assignments that will help you put each cardinal rule into practice. You'll be formulating your business battle plan as we go, so take notes! Let's begin.

LAYING THE GROUNDWORK FOR YOUR BATTLE PLAN

WHEN IT COMES TO FINDING your merchandise, you want to take a couple of things into consideration. First, you need to know what's trending. Hot new anime that explode in Japan and the US create plenty of fans looking to purchase merchandise and you need to be on top of it. Second, you need to know what other vendors are stocking (or not stocking) so you can shrink your search down to a manageable and focused group of exclusive products. And, finally, you need to be able to search for unique products by conducting effective product searches on Japanese sites.

So, what's the best way to gather this information? Well, the upcoming assignments will take you through several ways to find the information you need so you can start to identify the scope of merchandise you'll want to investigate further.

Here's what coming:

- Conduct online research on what's hot and what's not.
- Ferret out popular merchandise through fieldwork.
- Build variety into your merchandise plan.
- Google search the Japanese names of anime.

Let's get going!

ASSIGNMENT #1:
Conduct online research on what's hot and what's not

For this assignment, we'll focus on finding a list of what's trending by researching in-the-know websites. These provide a wealth of anime news from what's currently happening to what's going to happen. Even if you just glance at their homepages, you'll get a good idea about the hottest anime generating the most buzz.

STEP-BY-STEP INSTRUCTIONS:

1. Power on your computer and open your Internet browser. Enter crunchyroll.com in the address bar and go to the website.

2. Click on Shows in the menu bar.

3. The results: The most popular anime shows in the US are instantly revealed, including pictures of the main characters.

4. Now enter animenewsnetwork.com in the address bar and go to the website.

5. Click on Encyclopedia in the menu bar.

6. Click the Latest in Japan option under 'Anime.'

7. The results: The web page lists the popular anime series with upcoming TV and movie releases, which will utterly thrill their fans. Clicking on any name, will take you to another screen that reveals a wealth of information about the show.

8. There are many lists available on animenewsnetwork.com so take your time to thoroughly search this site. Other valuable information is found in the preview guides for the spring, summer, fall and winter television seasons. These guides, found under the 'New Anime' tab, give you a heads-up on what's going to be trending over the next several months.

9. Bookmark these websites and revisit them for news on what's trending as well as to pick up information about upcoming shows and their storylines. Another good site to bookmark is Funimation (funimation.com). It's another website full of the latest anime news.

These American websites are superb resources for anime news, but the best, most detailed and all-encompassing resources are the Japanese sites. Don't let the fact they're in Japanese scare you off from regularly visiting these sites for news.

Tackling the Japanese anime news websites involves a more sophisticated search. But these searches allow you to get the news directly from the horse's mouth, so to speak. The information needs to be translated into English, which you can do by pasting its URL into Translate Google (translate.google.com).

One good Japanese website is Charapedia (charapedia.jp/research/). They conduct a quarterly survey of 10,000 Japanese fans, asking them for the most anticipated anime series for the upcoming TV season. They use the results to rank the top twenty shows that fans are the most excited about. You can use their survey results to build your merchandise plan initially as well as add variety to your product mix in the future.

Charapedia also asks fans all sorts of imaginative questions in monthly surveys that produce top ten rankings in a range of categories. For example, they'll provide rankings for the most popular male, female, teacher, fighter, pet or other quirky characters. If you're stuck on which character's merchandise you want to stock, these questionnaires are another resource that can help you to gauge who's hot and who's not.

But there's more to your investigation than just the online resources. They say 'seeing is believing,' so the next assignment asks you to visit conventions with the intention of gathering more information that will kick the development of your merchandise plan into high gear.

ASSIGNMENT #2:
Ferret out popular merchandise through fieldwork

Most vendors are interested in anime and manga themselves and if that's the case with you too, this next assignment should be a lot of fun. What you want to do is plan to drop by a few dealer rooms at some upcoming conventions. Saturdays, during the late morning or early afternoon, are a good time to do this.

For this assignment, you're not only learning more about your customers but also what your fellow vendors are stocking at their booth. After all, they are the competition! Use them to learn what works, what doesn't and what merchandise they might be overlooking.

STEP-BY-STEP INSTRUCTIONS:

1. Visit a few dealer rooms and scope out the hot-selling items at different booths.

2. Don't be shy. Ask the vendors which anime series and items are selling the best. Photograph several popular booths so that you can remember the different items they had for sale. Also, photograph the merchandise at booths that are not busy at all. Attendees skip these booths because those vendors are failing to heed *Cardinal rule 1: Customer Con* and are not selling the anime or manga that customers *want* to buy.

3. Make a note of the price range for several of the popular merchandise categories. You'll need this information for a later assignment so take detailed notes. For example:

    - Pocket watches: $15 – $35
    - Small plushies: $8 – $20
    - Large plushies: $30 – $40
    - Posters and art: $8 – $15 or two for $20
    - T-shirts: $8 – $20

- Figures: $10 – $18 (smaller than 4 inches)
  $20 – $48 (4 to 10 inches)
  $50 and higher (limited edition or collectible)

4. Write down the most popular costumes worn by attendees.

   Record both the anime series and the character. If you're not sure, go ahead and ask the attendee the name of their character and from which anime. Convention-goers love to talk about their favorite characters and their dealer-room purchases. And don't forget to ask permission to take their picture.

5. Attend the costume contest.

   We learned in the customer backstory that fans spend a tremendous amount of time creating their costumes. The costume contest, even though it's a small sample size, provides another good reference point for which characters are popular.

As you are immersing yourself in finding out what's hot and what's not, you also have to learn to speak 'anime' by knowing the names of popular shows and characters. It's important to speak the language so you can converse with your customers and know what merchandise is going to be of interest to them. You'll be more credible, and able to do a better job convincing the customer to make a purchase. Attendees are more likely to buy from vendors who know what they're talking about.

For example, let's say you sell *Batman* merchandise. You should at least know:
- The plot summary – caped crusader who fights bad guys.
- The main characters – Batman, Robin, Joker, Harley Quinn and Commissioner Gordon, to name a few.

There are always a few attendees dressed as Harley Quinn at every convention. If you are selling *Batman* merchandise, you want to immediately know what items to discuss if 'Harley' stops by your booth. As you become familiar with the most popular and trending anime, you'll find speaking anime becomes second nature.

Harley leads us into another important consideration because she may not stop by any booth that sells *Batman* merchandise. At the convention, she may be searching for alpacas. Since Harley represents your target market, you'll want to have a variety of anime and items available at your booth to better your shot at appealing to her and others.

During your convention visits, did you observe most vendors selling items from several merchandise categories? Did you witness fans purchasing a variety of items from their favorite shows? Did you see at least one 'Walmart' vendor sprawled over three or more spaces? Did you notice most of their items collecting dust? Did you see vendors who didn't attract many, or even any, customers? How was the merchandise of the unpopular vendors different from the successful vendors? What were the most popular items purchased?

Even though I wasn't standing by your side for this assignment – I know the answer to the last question – figures, plushies, key chains and posters or art. The next assignment will help you to organize your notes and bring to the surface anime and items you should investigate further.

ASSIGNMENT #3:
Build variety into your merchandise plan

You need to make sure you have a good mix of popular products from several different anime in your merchandise plan. In this assignment, we'll organize your notes from your dealer room visits and accomplish three things: Identify what anime is popular, identify the most popular anime items, and find the anime gold mines barely touched by other vendors that are ripe for you to target as a niche opportunity.

STEP-BY-STEP INSTRUCTIONS:

1. Upload your photos of the vendor booths from the dealer rooms you visited in your previous assignment.

2. Select a vendor and dissect the items on sale at their booth. Use a separate sheet of paper or a spreadsheet to divide the key information into three columns. The first column contains the anime show, the second column lists the category of items related to the anime sold by the vendor, and the third column details the characters depicted by the item. For now, broad categories are fine.

3. Add to your list until you have broken down and detailed the product mixes of about twenty different vendors, including a few unsuccessful ones as a reminder to avoid these items and anime shows. This should be enlightening because you'll see a large number of vendors selling the same items from the same anime. You'll also spot anime where there are very few offerings by vendors – so put these on your 'investigate further' list. A sample of how to lay out your information is below:

Vendor Booth #1 Merchandise

Title	Category/Item	Characters
Pokémon	Plushies	Eevee, Umbreon, Pikachu, Pichu, Mew, Togepi
Various anime and movies characters	Funko Pop! figures	Seventy characters (one figure each from a multitude of shows and movies)
Attack on Titan, Sailor Moon, Naruto, Bleach, Sword Art Online, Evangelion	Wall scrolls	Several characters from each anime
League of Legends	Pendants, figures, weapons set	Vayne, Caitlyn, Lucian, Lee Sin, Yasuo, Thresh, Jinx, Blitzcrank, Shaco, Ekko

4. On a separate sheet of paper or in a spreadsheet, list the name of the anime shows, characters and items you *observed* most frequently being purchased by customers. For example, *Pokémon* Eevee plushies or *Batman* Funko POP! figures. Develop a top twenty-five list of the bestsellers based on your observations.

   By cross-checking both spreadsheets and finding the overlap, you now have a list of popular characters and items that merit further investigation. Later, you'll be able to search for different styles, poses or colors of these bestsellers, making *Cardinal rule 3: Think different* an actionable part of your process to build your merchandise plan.

5. Can you identify any gaps in what other vendors are offering? What about the costumes worn by attendees? Was there merchandise available from their shows at a number of vendors? You are looking for what is *not* being sold at the con so that you can fill the vacancy and exploit an underserved niche. Refer back to the crunchyroll list to see if any popular anime is largely being missed by other vendors. Then add these shows to your 'investigate further' list. Since most vendors don't invest the time to find pockets of opportunity, you'll unearth a gold mine of anime series that are under-represented. I always have at least three in my back pocket.

Studying your answers, analyzing your convention notes and reviewing the dealer room photos will reveal broad patterns of the most desired anime, characters and items. For instance, *League of Legends* may dominate the top five of highly-purchased items. Or you may see a more specific pattern, like *Pokémon* Pikachu plushies were highly sought after. You can use these patterns as a starting point in your search for distinctive merchandise with the aim of standing out from the vendor masses.

It is also time to shake any pre-existing notions from your head about the items you like and want to stock. If your favorite anime, manga, TV show or movie didn't make it onto any of your lists, it's best to enjoy them as a fan and abandon any further pursuit of them as a vendor.

In most cases, you will need to purchase unique or exclusive items of the bestsellers you identified from international suppliers, usually in Japan. The upcoming assignments help you find authentic Japanese items that will be the focal point of your merchandise plan.

ASSIGNMENT #4:
Google search the Japanese names of anime

Konnichiwa! Are you ready for a wild ride through Japan in search of unique items? This assignment will step you through exactly what you need to do. So, since we're going to be using Japanese websites and search engines to find and purchase products, you may be asking, 'Do I need to learn how to speak or read Japanese?' Well…

いいえあなたが日本語を読む必要はありません

Just kidding, the answer is no. You don't need to purchase Rosetta Stone, but you *must* conduct your product searches using the *Japanese name and spelling* of the anime series in question. Why? So the Japanese websites selling those items come up in your search results. Typing in English words will only fetch results from English-language stores, usually in the US.

The unique items you're seeking are going to be exclusively available in Japan. And Japanese suppliers list everything in the Japanese language. Makes sense, doesn't it? But don't quit on me now, because Internet searches in Japanese are a lot easier than they sound.

To get started, you only need to be able to find the Japanese name and spelling for anime shows. This is the only Japanese you'll need to know and a Google search easily uncovers the information. It's painless, I promise, and this assignment proves it.

The first thing to note is that the English names of anime series and the characters are frequently different from their original Japanese names. For example, the Japanese name for *Black Butler* is *Kuroshitsuji*.

Stay with me here … there's more.

Kuroshitsuji is the spelling of the show's Japanese name using the English alphabet, not the Japanese alphabet.

Still with me?

The show's name using the Japanese alphabet is 黒執事 (this is the Japanese spelling for *Kuroshitsuji*). You'll probably not be able to pronounce that! However, you can at least try to pronounce *Kuroshitsuji*.

Let's make sure you got that:

English name	Japanese name using English alphabet	Japanese name using Japanese alphabet
Black Butler	Kuroshitsuji	黒執事

The important takeaway here is that a Japanese name and Japanese alphabet spelling exist for each anime show. And you need to know the Japanese alphabet spelling to conduct effective searches. Your Japanese search results, when translated back to English, will simply refer to the anime using its Japanese name (i.e. *Kuroshitsuji*).

So let's practice a Google search for both of the Japanese names – using the English alphabet and the Japanese alphabet (which I often call 'squiggly lines').

STEP-BY-STEP INSTRUCTIONS:

1. Power on your computer, open your browser and go to **google.com**.

2. **Type** *Black Butler* in the search bar and click **search.**

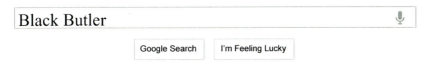

The results you'll get should look similar to this:

Black Butler - Wikipedia, the free encyclopedia
en.wikipedia.org/wiki/**Black_Butler**   Wikipedia
Black Butler (Japanese: 黒執事, Hepburn: Kuroshitsuji) is a manga written and illustrated by Yana Toboso. Since its debut on September 16, 2006, it has been...
List of Black Butler episodes - List of Black Butler characters - Hiro

SELLING TO HEROES, VILLAINS AND GEEKS

The Wikipedia search result usually appears on the first page and this is where I recommend you look. The first line lists the Japanese alphabet name (黒執事) for *Black Butler* and the Japanese name using the English alphabet (*Kuroshitsuji*). See, that was easy and took less than 0.18 seconds!

Many of the Japanese shows have their own Wikipedia page. The page will generally detail the show's name(s), the plot summary, character biographies, pictures and much more. You can visit Wikipedia to quickly learn the background of any anime or manga series. (Think of Wikipedia as your Cliff Notes for anime and manga.)

Let's practice once more by conducting a Google search for *Attack on Titan's Japanese name and spelling*.

1. Open a new window in your browser and go to **google.com**.

2. Type *Attack on Titan* in the search bar and click **search**.

The results you get will be similar to this:

Attack on Titan - Wikipedia, the free encyclopedia
en.wikipedia.org/wiki/**Attack_on_Titan** ▼   Wikipedia ▼

Attack on Titan (Japanese: 進撃の巨人, Hepburn: Shingeki no Kyojin, lit. "Advancing Giants") is a Japanese manga series written and illustrated by Hajime ...
Attack on Titan episodes - List of Attack on Titan characters - Hajime Isa

Wikipedia shows us that *Shingeki no Kyojin* is the Japanese name for *Attack on Titan* and also gives the Japanese alphabet version (進撃の巨人). That's all there is to it. This is the only Japanese you need to know for each anime to search for and buy products from Japan.

All you have to do is copy and paste the Japanese spelling (or squiggly lines) into a search engine when you conduct your initial search for products located in Japan. Painless, right? Up next, we're travelling to Japan to learn how to search and purchase anime items to populate your merchandise plan.

THE HUNT FOR MERCHANDISE

WE'VE TALKED EXTENSIVELY ABOUT FOCUSING your attention on Japan to find unique or exclusive anime merchandise. And, initially, product searches in a foreign language can consume a large amount of your time. And once you locate the items, the intricacies of the purchasing and shipping process can be daunting, at first. Persevere! I'm sure you've heard this wise statement about hard work paving the road to success, 'If it were completely easy from the get-go, everyone would do it.' So, be dogged in your determination to make your vendor business successful right out of the gate.

Believe me, it is worth the effort when you get it right. Be patient and push forward. Being successful takes creativity, unquenchable curiosity, risk and a willingness to learn. Don't be a scofflaw by ditching the hard work of research. The more you practice, the quicker you'll get it, and soon enough you'll be a pro.

The next several assignments will make you feel like you're learning on steroids. They include tasks to:

- Find unique items on Japanese sites.
- Master the Japanese auction bidding process.
- Understand the Japanese proxy service purchasing process and fees.

- Understand the Japanese proxy service shipping process and fees.
- Price your merchandise to sell fast.
- Investigate Chinese wholesalers (okay, we're no longer in Japan but we're still in Asia, heading 1,300 miles west).

Let's get started.

ASSIGNMENT #5:
Find unique items on Japanese sites

As we have discussed, Japan yields the best merchandise but learning the process for finding and purchasing your items *does* take patience. The easiest way to explain the big-picture purchasing process of buying items located in Japan is to compare it to buying stuff on Amazon. We'll look at how customers purchase items from a Japanese commerce website called *FromJapan* (fromjapan.co.jp) in contrast to how US customers buy stuff on Amazon.

Description of services

Amazon	FromJapan
You can find a vast number of American items for sale on Amazon. The buyer enters the name of the item in Amazon's search bar. The search results list all the US sellers for that item. Amazon's service connects buyers and sellers.	You can find a vast number of Japanese items for sale on FromJapan. The buyer enters the name of the item in FromJapan's search bar. The search results list all the Japanese sellers for that item. FromJapan's service connects buyers and sellers.
Amazon facilitates the purchasing process, collects the purchase price and forwards the funds to the seller for a fee (paid by the seller). The items are shipped by Amazon or the seller to the buyer's address.	FromJapan facilitates the purchasing process, collects the purchase price and forwards the funds to the seller for a fee (paid by the buyer). The items are shipped by FromJapan to the buyer's address.

The above description shows the similarity of the product search and purchase process between Amazon and FromJapan. You'll notice the only real difference is that the buyer pays the service fee for using FromJapan's services rather than the seller, and FromJapan handles all shipments to the buyer. In this assignment, we'll be discussing FromJapan's role as a commerce site to locate items for sale. In later assignments, we'll discuss how to purchase items listed on FromJapan through its proxy service in greater detail.

Whatever it is you want – arcade and rare Ichiban kuji prizes or newly-released anime items – FromJapan's search engine will locate all items that are for sale. And the good news is that the results are displayed in English or easily translated into English (read the next sensei tip for the translation disclaimer).

The FromJapan homepage (fromjapan.co.jp) is ground zero for the search process. It really is an Amazon-like website for Japanese products. Take it slow and follow the simple step-by-step instructions in this assignment. Let's stick with the *Black Butler* results from one of our previous Google searches to practice our first product search.

STEP-BY-STEP INSTRUCTIONS:

1. Open a new browser window and enter **fromjapan.co.jp** in the address bar. Go to the website.

2. In the upper left-hand corner on FromJapan's homepage, click on the **Categories** drop down arrow and then select **Comics Anime & Manga.**

3. Click on the **Japanese** language drop down arrow on the right and select **English.**

4. Go back to your earlier *Black Butler* Google search and find the Wikipedia result. Copy and paste the Japanese alphabet characters 黒執事 (squiggly lines) into FromJapan's search box. Ignore the instructions to 'type' in a key word. Just copy and paste the Japanese alphabet characters straight into this box.

> Please type in a keyword in Japanese! Example: キー・ワ

5. Click the **Search icon.** Search

6. **All of the** *Black Butler* items for sale (over 4,000) on Rakuten Global Market, the auction site Yahoo Japan, and other online stores will pop up.

7. Click on any item's link for a larger view of the item and click **Go to shopping site** for more detailed product information. The shopping site reveals the same type of information that is found on any online store in the US (such as pictures, price or opening bid, shipping cost, description and so on).

> **Sensei tip:** Sometimes things don't go as perfectly as they are programmed and FromJapan's translation software is no exception. If any of the pages are not being translated to English, you can copy and paste the URL into translate.google.com. To translate, click on the drop down arrow next to 'Detect language' and select 'Japanese.' On the right side of the page, 'Translate to English' should already be selected. All you have to do is click 'Translate' and the entire web page is translated for you.
>
> The translation results are so-so, but you'll only need a few words or a paragraph converted to English to clear most questions up. You'll get the hang of it and – believe me – one Japanese picture is worth a thousand English words.

Now, you're ready to search for items for sale from the anime on your 'investigate further' list.

8. Locate the Japanese alphabet spelling of the anime by doing a Google search and clicking on its Wikipedia page.

9. Repeat steps 4 -7 using your anime's name instead of *Black Butler*.

10. Open up a spreadsheet on your computer. This will be your practice worksheet for the remaining assignments. For this practice step, copy the URLs along with a brief description for a few of the items you are interested in possibly purchasing into the spreadsheet.

11. Repeat this search process for two more of the anime on your 'investigate further' list, copying the URL and description for three items from each anime into the practice spreadsheet.

> **Sensei tip:** Instead of clicking on every single link in the FromJapan search results, you can be guided by the pictures. They accurately portray the items for sale and it's the fastest way to scan through hundreds of items in minutes.

If you only want to search for a specific category of items for a particular anime, like figures, you may not want to wade through a bunch of stuff you're not interested in. The easiest way to narrow your search is to add the Japanese alphabet letters for the merchandise category (i.e. figures) to the end of the Japanese alphabet spelling of the show's name.

STEP-BY-STEP INSTRUCTIONS:

1. To continue with our *Black Butler* example, let's search for *Black Butler* figures. Go to **translate.google.com. Enter 'figure' in the left box and translate it into Japanese.**

English name	Japanese name using English alphabet	Japanese name using Japanese alphabet
Black Butler	Kuroshitsuji	黒執事
Black Butler figure	Kuroshitsuji figure	黒執事 フィギュア

   Plot twist: FromJapan's search engine is good, but filtering search results is not one of its strong points. It may not display any results by merchandise category. So, in order to search for items by category, such as *Black Butler* figures, you must trot over to each online store's website.

2. Go directly to Yahoo auction (auctions.yahoo.co.jp). Copy and paste the Japanese alphabet for *Black Butler* (黒執事) into the search bar. Also, copy and paste translate.google's Japanese alphabet for 'figure' (フィギュア) to the end of the name (see below). Even though the website is in Japanese, it's easy to locate the search bar by looking for the magnifying glass symbol.

3. Click the magnifying glass to begin the search.

4. All of the *Black Butler* figures currently for sale will appear in the search results. You can translate the search results into English by pasting the URL into translate.google.com.

5. Repeat these steps to narrow your search for items sold by category for your anime and enter the URL of items that pique your interest into your practice spreadsheet.

Translate.google.com may provide several Japanese translation suggestions for different categories of merchandise so use my answer key below to select the right spelling.

Merchandise category	*Japanese alphabet spelling*
Figure	フィギュア
Plushies Stuffed Stuffed animals	ぬいぐるみ
Pocket Watch	懐中時計
Lottery (to find lottery prizes for an anime show)	一番くじ
Key chain	キーホルダー
Key chain (alternative spelling when placed in front of the title of the anime)	キーチェーン
Charms (similar to key chains)	チャーム
Rubber strap (similar to key chains)	ラバーストラップ
Wall scroll	タペストリー
Poster	ポスター

The number of anime items for sale will vary based on the popularity and age of the manga or anime series. Newer shows have fewer items available unless they're a massive hit. You'll also find slim pickings for merchandise for popular series in season one of their TV broadcast. Entertainment companies gear up their product release schedule once the new shows prove they have staying power.

Once you've done all your preliminary research, you'll have a pretty clear idea about what merchandise you want to add to your final merchandise plan. So next up, you'll complete a short assignment on the auction bidding process, Japanese style. It's so similar to eBay that you'll breeze through this assignment in no time.

ASSIGNMENT #6:
Master the Japanese auction bidding process

The Yahoo Japan auction site (auctions.yahoo.co.jp) – where most of the arcade and Ichiban kuji prizes are sold – functions just like eBay. When you click on an auction link, it shows you all of the information you need, including:

- Auction beginning date and time. The 24-hour clock method more commonly referred to as 'military time' is the conventional time format displayed.
- Auction ending date and time.
- Days and hours remaining in the auction.
- Minimum bid price in yen.
- Number of bids made.
- Buy-it-now price (if applicable).
- Product condition (new, used or second-hand).
- Item description: The item's origin (such as arcade, lottery or newly-released), size (in centimeters) and domestic shipping cost.
- Keep in mind that all of the item prices are stated in yen. The Japanese yen abbreviates as JPY and ¥ is the international symbol, and 円 is the symbol used within the country of Japan.

Japan currency conversion
(approximate)

¥1 (yen)	=	$0.01 US currency
¥100	=	1 US dollar
¥500	=	5 US dollars
¥1,000	=	10 US dollars

I use a rough currency exchange rate (like the one above) to calculate in two seconds the price in US dollars for items listed. To find up-to-the-minute exchange rates, simply Google 'convert yen to dollars' and input the yen amount in the currency calculator that comes up. Traditionally, the exchange rate fluctuates within a fairly narrow range unless the stock market crashes.

You'll see many listings for Yahoo Japan auction in your FromJapan (fromjapan.co.jp) search engine results. And this site is where we'll focus our attention to source unique products at bargain prices.

Assignment #5 taught you how to search for anime items using FromJapan's search engine or by going directly to Yahoo auction. Now we'll learn the best way to select the best auctions by walking through one of my auction experiences. Let's continue with *Black Butler* as our anime and search for an auction selling pocket watches. I find the following listing, click on the link or picture and see this (once it's translated to English):

In this particular example, three brand new *Black Butler* watches – Ciel, Sebastian and Krell – are being auctioned. (If you're not sure of the importance of the characters, you can revisit the Wikipedia page and check them out.) The minimum opening bid is 400 yen (or about $4) for all three watches. All three watches can be purchased immediately at the 'buy it now' price of 3,000 yen (or about $30). Six days remain on the auction and currently nobody has placed a bid. The description of the watches (which you can't see in the picture) states that they're brand new arcade prizes.

If I were going to place a bid, my maximum bid would be about 1,500 yen (or $15). If my maximum bid were the highest at the close of the auction, I would win three pocket watches for $15 or $5 per watch, excluding shipping and all other fees. But the winning bid could potentially be as low as 400 yen (or $4) for all three watches ($1.33 each) if no one else bids. The convention price at my booth would be $35 each because these watches are strictly limited to Japanese distribution via arcade games. They are manufactured by SEGA and are of the highest quality. No other vendor will be selling these particular watches and they will look very different from any other *Black Butler* watches sold at conventions. Now, it's your turn to select a few items on your practice spreadsheet and fill in more information to help with your purchasing decision.

STEP-BY-STEP INSTRUCTIONS:

1. Copy & paste the URL of a Yahoo auction item on your practice spreadsheet into your browser and go to the website.

2. Fill in the opening or current bid and the date the auction ends on your practice spreadsheet. Note: Yahoo limits the listing duration to a maximum of seven days. If the item does not sell, the seller can keep relisting the item but only in seven day increments.

3. Repeat steps 1 and 2 for each item on your practice spreadsheet.

Here are several tips to keep in mind when you are evaluating which auctions to add or keep on your practice spreadsheet:

Sensei tip: The *secret t*o getting the best bargain is to bid on auctions with *multiple items* available in a *single auction*. Aim for ones with three, thirty or even eighty items. For example, take a look at this auction I won for *Kuroko no basuke* lottery items as an example of this 'sensei tip' in action. There were about sixty items consisting of plushies, figures, key chains, buttons, posters and color folders in a single auction.

The winning bid was ¥9,800 or approximately $98 for sixty items. Yea! When you breakdown the cost per item, it averaged $1.63 for brand new merchandise that was distributed through the Ichiban kuji. Later, I sold these items for ten times more than the amount I paid. (We'll discuss convention prices and potential profit in assignment #9.)

 Sensei tip: Ichiban kuji (lottery) and arcade prize values increase significantly over short periods of time due to limited distribution and quantities. Therefore, buy these items immediately when they appear in Yahoo auction or FromJapan's search engine results if they're part of your merchandise plan.

You should only consider an auction with just three items if the future convention price will exceed $30 per item, such as the *Black Butler* pocket watch example. Also, bidding on a few single item auctions is fine, but the majority of your auctions should have multiple items to ensure you get the best bargains.

Once you've found the hot merchandise you want to stock, it's time to learn the steps necessary to complete your purchases through a proxy service.

ASSIGNMENT #7:

Understand the Japanese proxy service purchasing process and fees

Stop. Before going any further, count to ten and take several deep breaths. When you purchase items from Japanese sellers, the orders are submitted to service providers such as FromJapan, which act as a proxy purchasing service. So before hitting FromJapan's 'buy now' button, you need to understand this kind of purchasing process in a bit more detail. It'll make things much easier when you're calculating the total costs involved for each purchase.

The first thing to understand is that you can't purchase products from the sellers directly; you have to go through FromJapan. Despite Japan's high tech reputation, very few Japanese sites are set up to accommodate global e-sales. Online shops in Japan do not have a convenient payment system, such as PayPal, where shipment information is transmitted to the seller. Foreign credit cards are not accepted and payments occur through wire transfers via Japanese banks.

Added to this, the business transactions are completed via email – in Japanese. Because Google's English to Japanese translation is so-so, it hinders the Japanese sellers' ability to conduct international business. The other thing to be aware of is that most Japanese sellers do not ship items outside of Japan.

But these stumbling blocks are easily navigated by companies, such as FromJapan, that offer a proxy purchasing service. It's called proxy purchasing because every order is proxy paid by the service provider. They pay the seller on the buyer's behalf. Simply put, for a percentage of the total price, a proxy service takes care of the hard work, including:

- Purchasing items from stores or individual sellers.
- Bidding on auctions.
- Communicating with sellers.
- Paying sellers.
- Receiving items at their warehouse in Japan.
- Packing and shipping items to international buyers.

All communication and business transactions between the proxy purchasing company and you will be conducted in English. And further, every form of payment is accepted, so it's quite easy to complete your transactions.

Why FromJapan?

FromJapan (fromjapan.co.jp) gets my highest recommendation. Their search engine is excellent. This system works seamlessly with Yahoo auction and it makes purchasing items from other websites a no-brainer. Their automated customer service emails are fantastic and keep you up-to-date on when your items arrive in their warehouse.

Other services that FromJapan provides include:

- Bundling all purchased items into one shipment. An individual item's shipping cost drops dramatically when more items ship at the same time. Any purchases made within a thirty-day window (the clock starts ticking when the first item arrives at the Japan warehouse) can be grouped together and shipped at the same time.

- Free storage of your purchases for the first thirty days.

- If you don't understand Google's Japanese to English translation, FromJapan will translate for you; just ask via the contact form. They usually reply within twenty-four hours during the week.

- International shipping discounts of up to ten percent for customers who reach certain spending thresholds.

- Periodic promotions that knock five percent off the purchase price of any item.

- Email alerts about new anime and manga product releases and Ichiban kuji prizes.

Aside from the great service they provide, FromJapan also has the cheapest fees of all the proxy purchasing service companies. Fees are always a complicated matter (especially the unexpected ones) to calculate exactly, but I'll give you a basic rundown.

Each order has a minimum commission fee of 200 yen ($2) and a system fee of five percent of the total purchase price. On top of this, there is a bank transfer fee, another five percent system-usage fee and additional fees where applicable. It sounds worse than it is! Let's go back to the earlier *Black Butler* pocket watch example to examine these fees:

Note: Yen to US dollar conversions are approximate.

		Yen	USD
1	Item price/winning bid	¥1,500	$15.00
2	FJ commission fee	¥200	$2.00
3	FJ system usage fee [(1 + 2) x 5%]	¥85	$0.85
4	**Sub-total (1 + 2 + 3)**	**¥1,785**	**$17.85**
5	Domestic delivery charge	¥700	$7.00
6	FJ bank transfer fee	¥172	$1.72
7	Overseas shipping	¥900	$9.00
8	**Sub-total (5 + 6 + 7)**	**¥1,772**	**$17.72**
9	**FJ system usage fee [8 x 5%]**	**¥89**	**$0.89**
	Total cost all 3 watches (4 + 8 + 9)	¥3,646	$36.46
	Convention price	\$35 per watch	

The total FromJapan fees are ¥374 (2 + 3 + 9) or $3.74. FromJapan handles paying the seller through the Japanese banking system, which charges ¥172 per transaction. The seller, like in the US, determines the domestic delivery charge for shipping the item from the seller's location to the FromJapan warehouse. In the above example, the domestic delivery charge is ¥700. The pocket watches' overseas shipping cost to the US is ¥900. But the pocket watches were not shipped by themselves. They were packed and shipped as part of a much larger shipment of items, so the ¥900 is their portion of the shipping cost. We'll get into the specifics of bundling shipments to keep shipping cost low in the next assignment. For now, let's finish the discussion on the *Black Butler* pocket watch example.

At this point, the acquisition cost for the three pocket watches started at $15.00 (winning bid) but, with proxy fees and shipping, the true cost is $36.46 for all three watches.

The convention revenue generated from the sale of all three watches will be $105 (3 x $35 price per watch). And yes, I've successfully sold these watches for $35 apiece. This example reinforces the earlier 'sensei tip' to only bid on auctions that include multiple items. This allows proxy fees and other costs to be spread out over a number of items instead of one item bearing the full brunt of the proxy and shipping cost.

To recap, these are the kind of fees you'll generally be hit with when using FromJapan. You can go to fromjapan.co.jp/title/charge?lang=en for a detailed explanation of their fee schedule. Also, if you're unsure of the total cost of an item, you can always ask FromJapan for a cost quote before making your purchase.

FromJapan's costs are cheaper than other proxy purchasing service companies such as Noppin.com, Buyee.jp and shoppingmalljapan.com. These other companies charge a flat fee between ten to fifteen percent of the purchase price. However, there are other hidden costs such as the PayPal transaction or bank wire transfer fees not specified on their webpage. Also, they may not economically pack your items for overseas shipping and this is a big 'no-no' – as you'll see in the upcoming assignment. When it's all said and done, FromJapan is your best bet for paying the lowest fees possible.

Sensei tip: Just like Amazon, you must have a FromJapan account to use their service. To register for a free account, go to fromjapan.co.jp and follow the standard sign-up process.

Now that we've walked through why you need to use a proxy purchasing service, their benefits and fees, I'll walk you briefly through the steps to purchase items through FromJapan. BUT YOU SHOULD NOT PLACE ANY BIDS OR ORDERS UNTIL YOU COMPLETE YOUR MERCHANDISE AND BUSINESS BATTLE PLANS (assignments #11 and #12). We're still in practice mode.

STEP-BY-STEP INSTRUCTIONS:

1. Complete the free registration process to open a FromJapan account (fromjapan.co.jp).

2. Enter **fromjapan.co.jp/title/service?lang=en** in the address bar of your browser. Click on the **Auction Service Guide Section** heading.

3. Read through the step-by-step instructions for the 'Auction Bidding Service' and 'Shopping Service.' The information is so beautifully laid out on this page that there is no need to repeat the information here. The instructions are detailed and clear and the webpage provides links to each FromJapan page necessary to complete your transaction. All you need is the item's URL. If you get stuck anywhere in the process, FromJapan's customer service can provide assistance.

4. Copy the URL of the Yahoo auction item you wish to bid on and then paste it into FromJapan's order form (fromjapan.co.jp/auction?lang=en). You'll see the step-by-step online instructions to submit your bid. We won't proceed any further since this assignment is to only get you familiar with FromJapan's purchasing process.

5. To place an order from an online store, click on the **Place an order (Shopping)** button and copy the URL into the space provided at the bottom of the page. Again, the step-by-step instructions to submit your order are very straightforward.

Before placing a bid or order, you must 'place a deposit' with FromJapan for the entire purchase price or your maximum bid. The amount of deposit will have to include FromJapan's 200 yen commission plus their system fee (5% of the purchase price) for each order. (The remaining fees are due when you're ready to ship the items to the US.) For auctions, if your winning bid is lower than your maximum bid, you will be refunded the difference. If for some reason the item is not purchased (i.e. store is out-of-stock) or you are not the winning bidder, you'll be refunded the purchase price only. FromJapan's fees are non-refundable.

You will repeat the above steps over and over again once you are 100% satisfied with your merchandise and business battle plans.

To keep cost to a minimum and preserve as much profit as possible, here are a few other tips when using a proxy service company:

- For online store purchases, keep the shipping cost low by purchasing a minimum of four of the same item from the same store. The domestic delivery charges can add up if you're only purchasing single items from many different sellers. It would be the same as ordering one item from four different online stores in the US – you would pay four different shipping costs.

- Purchase multiple items from the same seller at the same time. FromJapan stops charging the ¥200 commission when you place more than five orders with the same seller. For example, if you find an online store where you're interested in buying six different items, you'll only be charged the ¥200 commission on the first five orders.

- Use FromJapan's 'contact' form to ask the seller for the domestic shipping cost if it's not clearly stated on the item's webpage.

- When you place an order through FromJapan, the online form asks your shipping preference for the domestic delivery to FromJapan's warehouse. Choose the inexpensive second option – domestic shipping method without insurance and tracking. Japan's post office faithfully delivers packages from sellers to FromJapan's warehouse and there is no need to pay for tracking, insurance or express delivery services.

FromJapan's customer service runs smoothly so don't hesitate to contact them when you have questions.

The next assignment examines another aspect to consider when pursuing unique products from Japan for your vendor business – and it is *critical*. You'll learn how to keep your international shipping cost as low as possible.

ASSIGNMENT #8:
Understand the Japanese proxy service shipping process and fees

'KaBoom!' It is way too easy to blow your entire profit on shipping costs if you don't manage the quantity, size and weight of the items you ship from Japan to the US. Your packages have to travel almost 7,000 miles to reach the US border and it is this postage expense, not the item's price or proxy commission and fees, that you have to expertly manage. We'll go step-by-step and leave no stone unturned.

If you are using FromJapan, they will charge the actual shipping cost multiplied by the five percent 'system usage fee.' The shipping cost per item rises or falls dramatically based on the number of items, size and weight of each shipment. I can't stress the point strongly enough that you must consider these three factors when purchasing merchandise.

When purchasing items in Japan, it's important to buy large quantities to justify the international shipping cost. As a general rule of thumb, the more items shipped at the same time, the lower the shipping cost per item.

Let's look at an example to better understand how bundling items (i.e. shipping multiple purchases at the same time) can impact your cost to ship items to the US:

- Three auctions (as pictured below) totaling 175 items were successfully purchased on auctions.yahoo.co.jp. All three auctions were bundled together and shipped at the same time from Japan to the US.

- The shipment includes *Kuroko no basuke* plushies, figures, key chains, postcards, micro towels, posters, buttons, clear file folders and pencil cases. Everything is shipped in one large box.

- The international shipping cost is 18,400 yen. This shipping cost is the fee charged by Japan's post office to ship this package to the US. Their international postage service, called Express Mail Service (EMS), will be the cheapest option for shipments weighing up to 30kg.

Can you calculate the shipping cost per item?

Auction 1   Auction 2   Auction 3

Let's break it down.

STEP-BY-STEP INSTRUCTIONS:

1. Divide the overseas shipping cost of 18,400 yen by the 175 items in the shipment The shipping cost per item calculates to 105 yen (or $0.91 by the exact current exchange rate)

But the shipping cost isn't the only fee. Besides the actual purchase price of the merchandise, plan to pay for several additional costs to complete the business transaction in Japan. Your FromJapan invoice will detail the different categories of fees. In our example, the purchase price was paid at the time of purchase, so the remaining charges on the FromJapan invoice looked like this:

	Total number of purchases	3 orders (175 items)
	Weight/size (1 package)	13.17 kg – 53 cm x 50 cm x 47 cm
1	Domestic delivery charges	800 yen
2	Bank transfer fees	270 yen
3	Sales tax	2,304 yen
4	Overseas shipping	18,400 yen
5	Box fee (new)	500 yen
6	Total (1 - 5)	22,274 yen
7	System usage fee (6 x 5%)	1,114 yen
	Total charges (6 +7)	**23,388 yen ($202.59*)**

(* The exact currency exchange rate at the time of this transaction was 1 yen = USD$0.008662.)

SELLING TO HEROES, VILLAINS AND GEEKS

2. The above example shows the total charge is 23,388 yen by adding the other fees (domestic delivery charge, bank transfer fee, sales tax, box fee, system usage fee) onto the overseas shipping cost. Divide the total charge by the number of items (23,388 yen/175 items) in the shipment.

The additional cost per item - above and beyond the purchase price - is 134 yen or $1.16 when you add in overseas shipping and all of the proxy fees. The $1.16 is the amount you'll add to the purchase price for each individual item as part of the item's total acquisition cost.

This example lays out all the costs you can expect when using a proxy purchasing service. The main cost, though, is surprisingly not the item's price nor the proxy fees but the overseas shipping. The shipping cost per item for this example was unusually low because the number of items in two out of the three auctions was huge (60+). Also, they were small and light-weight. This is the secret to keeping your shipping cost per item low, so I am shouting it from the rooftops: SELECT AUCTIONS WITH MUTIPLE ITEMS AND BUNDLE YOUR SHIPMENTS.

Typically, my shipping cost averages between $3 and $5 per item. And since my convention prices average $20 and higher, like the *Black Butler* pocket watches, the profit margins are attractive – which we're getting ready to discuss in the next assignment.

3. Go back to your spreadsheet and add a column for the proxy service fees and your estimated international shipping cost – about $4 *per item* is a good, conservative starting point. Calculate the total acquisition cost for each item by adding the estimated purchase price, proxy fees and international shipping cost.

Sensei tip: Be realistic about an item's purchase price versus the final delivered cost. Transaction fees, shipping and proxy purchasing fees all add up.

Your packages will arrive at your address within seven to ten days after FromJapan notifies you that your items have been shipped and their email will include the tracking number. They are delivered by the United States Postal Service (USPS). To track the progress of your shipment, you can go to USPS's tracking website (tools.usps.com).

Mastering the concept behind this assignment is so important because the total cost of purchasing an item is the springboard for determining the convention price that will bring you maximum profit. And now that we have dispatched with the cost information for purchasing and shipping merchandise, we can turn our attention to setting convention prices. We'll discover how to determine the convention price as well as the potential profit in the next assignment.

ASSIGNMENT #9:
Price your merchandise to sell fast

Developing an eye for which items will be profitable is contingent on three factors:

- The likelihood of selling the items at conventions (based on your customer research and *Cardinal rule 1: Customer Con*).
- The purchase price including proxy commission, fees and shipping.
- The convention price you establish for the items (based on competitive alternatives and *Cardinal rule 4: Avoid customer price shock*).

We know items that fall within the popular merchandise categories and are based on popular anime will have a high likelihood of selling well at conventions. And the previous assignments have shown you how to estimate the actual purchase price of items sourced from Japan. So that leaves us with learning how to set appropriate convention prices for your items that match the customer's perceived value, while squeezing out every ounce of profit for your business. This assignment walks through an example of how to make this determination.

What is the standard price range?

When you are looking to set your convention prices, the best place to start is to look at similar items already being sold at conventions. You'll notice standard convention price points for many items and can use them as a reference. Your fieldwork notes on prices from *Assignment #2* are essential for this task. To get you started, I've listed some standard price ranges by category. Obviously, I can't swear to the universality of the prices provided here, but I bet they're pretty close to this:

- Pocket watches: $15 – $35
- Small plushies: $8 – $20
- Large plushies: $30 – $40
- Figures: $10 – $18 (smaller than 4 inches)
  $20 – $48 (4 to 10 inches)
  $50 and higher (limited edition or collectible)

- Posters and art: $8 – $15 or two for $20
- T-shirts: $8 – $20
- Hats: $15 – $30
- Backpacks: $15 – $25
- Key chains: $8 – $18
- Jewelry: $8 – $20
- Box sets: $15 – $45 (Four or more pieces of key chains, rings, necklaces or pendants)

I've noticed that plushies have a wide price range but they tail off at the $75 mark. When setting prices for these items, my criterion is to look at the size and popularity of the character. The bigger the size or the more popular the character – the higher the price can be. Also, the price of figures covers the gamut from a few dollars to a couple of hundred, so these are the trickiest prices to get right. You really need to study other vendor prices to determine the right price for the type of figure you'll be selling.

What is the item's perceived value?

Let's look back at my *Black Butler* pocket watch example. Pocket watch prices at conventions range from $15 to $35. I sell mine for $35, which is at the top end of the range. But I'm the only vendor who carries these particular watches, they are authentic Japanese merchandise and *Black Butler* merchandise is under-represented at conventions, so the price is justified.

Keep in mind that the uniqueness of the item is what gives you the flexibility to set the price at the high end of the standard range. Let's have some fun and visualize this from the customer's viewpoint. Note the prices of these toy storm troopers offered by five different vendors:

$35   *$20*   *$20*   *$20*   *$20*

SELLING TO HEROES, VILLAINS AND GEEKS

It makes sense that customers will pay the higher price of $35 for something that looks different to what the other four vendors are selling. It's the only one available and everyone else is selling the exact same thing. This underscores the principle of uniqueness and exclusiveness, as discussed in the cardinal rules, as a means to attract customers and charge a higher price for your merchandise.

Will the mark-up be profitable?

Before purchasing your items, you need to make sure that the convention price falls within the range customers are willing to pay, and you will be able to apply a mark-up that covers your costs *and* provides a nice profit for you.

Let's review the definition of mark-up to ensure we're on the same page. The mark-up is the difference between the total cost of acquiring the item and its convention sales price. It is added onto all costs incurred in purchasing the item to allow for a profit for you. The retail mark-up is commonly calculated as the difference between the acquisition price and retail price (or convention price in our case) and is stated as a percentage.

The formula used to calculate this percentage is:

$$[(\text{Convention price} - \text{Acquisition price}) / \text{Acquisition price}] \times 100$$

$$= \text{Mark-up \%}$$

First up, we need to establish one very important ground rule. All convention prices will be marked up *at least* 100%. This is a pretty standard industry practice. A 100% mark-up rule is a good starting point but you really want to strive to get closer to 150% where possible. Some items can be marked up more than this, sometimes much more, and some will be marked up less. Your chief goal is to generate as much profit as possible on each item.

So, going back to our *Black Butler* pocket watch example, we purchased three watches for $36.46 inclusive of all costs. This means each watch cost $12.15. The convention price of each watch is $35.

Let's work out what the mark-up is using the formula described above:

$$[(\text{Convention price} - \text{Acquisition price}) / \text{Acquisition price}] \times 100$$
$$[(\$35 - \$12.15) / \$12.15] \times 100$$
$$= 188\%$$

The mark-up for each watch is 188%. Very good! For every watch sold, my gross profit is $22.85 (convention price minus acquisition price). However, the convention fees and other business expenses must be deducted from the gross profit of your total sales during a convention weekend, so this $22.85 is not pure profit.

Let's grab one of the *Kuroko no basuke* Yahoo auctions from *Assignment #8* and determine their convention prices and calculate the mark-up. The convention prices we'll set for these items can fall near the upper end of the range of similar items found at other vendor booths because the items are authentic Japanese merchandise, unique and exclusively available at your booth.

Auction 3

Acquisition price*:	¥7,912 or $66.41		
Convention prices:	11 figures @ $18 each	=	$198
	1 key chain	=	$10
	1 GAKUEN pencil bag	=	$12
	1 plush key chain	=	$14
Potential sales:		=	$234
Mark-up percentage [($234 − $66.41) / $66.41] x 100		=	252%

*Acquisition price includes the winning auction bid (¥5,701), the proxy service commission, the fees and the shipping costs.

The potential gross profit from all of these items amounts to $167.59 (the convention prices minus the acquisition costs). Not bad! And this is a real-life example from my business. I sold everything from this auction as well as the other two *Kuroko no basuke* auctions at these prices.

Your assignment:

1. At this stage, you may find your notes on item pricing aren't as detailed as you would like, or perhaps you haven't made it to enough dealer rooms yet. Either way, now is the time to hit some more dealer rooms and capture the detailed item prices charged by your future competition.

2. Take a second look at all of the unique items on your practice spreadsheet you were thinking about purchasing. Add a column on your spreadsheet for the convention price and guestimate each item's convention price based on the standard price range.

3. Calculate the gross profit and the mark-up percentage on each item. See if the purchase makes financial sense based on the mark-up you can apply.

Remember to keep your prices within the ballpark of other vendors' comparable items so that your merchandise moves quickly. You'll rapidly become an expert at determining which unique items will deliver the most profit. And since profit is partly derived from low acquisition cost, you should devote a substantial amount of your time hunting for bargains.

Sensei tip: To quickly calculate the minimum price you can charge using a 100% mark-up, you simply double the estimated cost (including shipping) of the item. If the answer falls within the normal convention price range for that item, you have the green light to go ahead and make the purchase.

You'll find plenty of bargains when purchasing authentic Japanese merchandise if you take the time to search for the best deal. And there are other options too. If you are interested in purchasing from Chinese wholesalers, the purchasing process is straightforward and this makes our next assignment simple and quick.

ASSIGNMENT #10:
Investigate Chinese wholesalers

Nǐ hǎo. On a scale of one to ten, the ease of purchasing from Chinese wholesalers rates an eight. It is much simpler than the process we looked at for Japanese purchases made through a proxy purchasing service. The only reason they don't score a ten is because of the language barrier. Some wholesalers use Google translate, which we already know is so-so. But, fortunately, communication is generally limited to 'Thank you for your order,' 'Your package has shipped,' and 'Here is your tracking number.'

And since we've already had the legitimate versus bootleg merchandise debate, we won't rehash it here. I'm not making any judgments; I'm simply providing the relevant information you need to make an informed decision about what you choose to stock at your booth.

Chinese websites are set up for English-speaking customers and the anime shows are typically listed by their American names, such as *Black Butler, Attack on Titan, Naruto, Dragon Ball, Final Fantasy*, and so on. If for some reason you can't find a particular anime show, then you can try searching for the Japanese name. For example, *Black Butler* may be listed as *Kuroshitsuji* or *Attack on Titan* as *Shingeki no Kyojin*. If you don't know the Japanese name, visit Wikipedia like we practiced earlier. But you probably won't need to do this in most cases.

Once you've found the merchandise you are looking for, the Chinese buying process works exactly the same as for online US stores, except they're located in China. The prices are even listed in US dollars – so you can pack away your currency exchange-rate calculator.

Every wholesaler sells several hundred anime items and most items you'll see listed are sourced from the same Chinese manufacturers regardless of which wholesaler you buy from. The items are identical but the prices can vary by a few pennies to a few dollars. You can rummage through one website and uncover 446 *Evangelion* items while another only offers 130. It's best to have a good idea about what you're looking for so you don't spend umpteen hours deciding which one of the thirty versions of an anime's backpack you want to purchase.

You'll also find enterprising Chinese individuals who sell the same merchandise from the same manufacturers. You'll start to recognize the same pictures on different websites. Also, the prices listed by the individual sellers are strongly competitive with the wholesaler prices.

The 'legit' wholesalers will accept PayPal or US credit cards, so you can have some confidence, and recourse if needed, when you make purchases. They usually don't have a minimum order requirement but you can check the website's 'FAQ' or 'How to order' tabs to locate this information. While you will come across some wholesalers that only deal with retail stores, there are plenty that sell to individuals. Also, you'll find a few websites that require you to register with them to view their wholesale prices.

So, let's have a go at searching for products from Chinese wholesalers.

STEP-BY-STEP INSTRUCTIONS:

1. Power on your computer and open your Internet browser and go to google.com.

2. Type 'anime wholesalers' in the Google search bar and click search.

3. A list of wholesaler websites will pop up in the search results.

If you're leery about placing an order, make sure the wholesaler accepts payment through PayPal. You'll be covered by PayPal's purchase protection when you pay for your merchandise.

Sensei tip: If you place an order with a supplier you've never used before, start with an amount less than $200. You want to be satisfied that the merchandise passes *your* quality standards before making a major investment in it.

If you have any questions about the purchase process, be proactive and email the wholesaler your questions. Queries are answered within twenty-four hours, but don't forget there is a twelve to fifteen hour time difference between China and the US. Also, since English is their second language or Google translate substitutes as the interpreter, you'll need to be patient if their answers are a little choppy. I recommend you be specific and detailed in your communications without being long-winded. And don't use contractions (for example use 'do not' instead of 'don't'). Contractions screw up the Google translation, which is another reason why it's only so-so.

What about shipping costs from China?

Chinese shipping costs to the US are notably cheaper than shipments from Japan. The cheaper cost has something to do with government subsidies, treaties and labor cost. But whatever the actual reason, US customers reap the benefit.

The supplier will always calculate the cheapest shipping method and provide you with options based on your timing needs. The shipping methods available include Express Mail Service (EMS), DHL, FEDEX and UPS. The EMS service equates to USPS Priority Mail International and has the same service benefits and features such as tracking and two-day delivery once the package arrives in the US and clears customs. Other cheaper shipping methods are available, such as Surface Air Lifted (SAL), but they have extended delivery times, inconvenient custom-clearance procedures and no tracking numbers. Every now and then, a wholesaler may suggest this option, but I recommend you politely decline. The meager savings aren't worth the headache.

International shipping can be as low as $1.50 and up to $4 per item depending on the number and weight of the items shipped. Once again, the larger the quantity you order, the lower the shipping cost will be per item. Let me drive this point home: The quantity of items shipped will have the biggest impact on your shipping costs. Seek to order a minimum of sixty items per shipment to reap the full benefit of a lower shipping cost per item. High shipping costs can smack the profit right out of the words 'gross profit.'

Oops alert: A friend of mine sent me an email complaining about the shipping cost for an order he placed with a Chinese wholesaler. Previously, I had combined his alpaca order (eight items) with my much larger alpaca order (sixty-seven items) from the same wholesaler so we could both enjoy the benefit of lower shipping costs per item. Both his items and mine were delivered in one shipment to my address. I specifically explained to him that the reason his shipping cost per item was so low ($1.89) was because his order was part of a larger shipment.

> He was thrilled with his items and the shipping cost and later decided to place a second order on his own for twenty-five items. In that instance the cost of shipping each item was $3.96, which was a huge increase versus the earlier cost. The twenty-five items he ordered comprised too small an order to achieve the lower rate per item he benefited from when our orders were combined.

But what if you only need twenty-five items and not sixty or so? Well, you have two options here: Wait until you can order a larger quantity or accept the fact that the shipping rate per item will be higher on a smaller shipment. You'll also need to accept that your gross profit will be lower for that shipment because of this. Charging higher prices will be the only way to maintain your profit margin.

One final point about purchasing items from Chinese wholesalers – avoid figures. Trust me, customers will notice the cheap quality. They want authentic Japanese figures. Once a customer has been burned by a vendor selling cheap knock-offs, they're determined not to let that happen again. In fact, they often promise to purchase my authentic figures if I will break the box seal so they can take a closer look at the quality and confirm its authenticity.

Making purchases from Chinese wholesalers is easy, cheap and expedient. However, these suppliers sell a lot of bootleg merchandise and it's not exclusive or unique.

> **Sensei tip:** US wholesalers and retailers may also make your list of suppliers. If you're looking for a particular item, Google search it in English. You may find a US supplier selling it at a low everyday price or otherwise running a sale.

> **Sensei tip:** Do not purchase items from yesasia.com. According to their rules, they are allowed to add exorbitant charges to your final price based on a mysterious formula only known to them. Therefore, the listed purchase price of items is extremely misleading.

Taobao

We previously touched on Taobao.com as another source for convention merchandise. It's another Amazon-like website for products sold by Chinese sellers and the prices are dirt cheap. However, walking you through the complicated Chinese search and purchasing process for Taobao is too complex to include in this book and is best communicated through my YouTube tutorial. Once you've cruised through several conventions, hop over to animevendor.com for a lesson in Taobao product searches. Click on the 'Members' tab and enter the code 'anime' for a visual assignment that walks you through step-by-step instructions for using Taobao.

So, at this stage, you've done your due diligence regarding your vendor business and completing all of the assignments will have helped clear a lot of things up. You're confident in your hot pursuit of merchandise that meets all of the bestseller criteria. Up next, you'll put everything in writing to provide guideposts for your ongoing business decisions.

THE NUTS AND BOLTS OF YOUR BATTLE PLAN

STRAP ON YOUR THINKING CAP because it's time to bang out your merchandise and business plans. At the end of these next two assignments, you'll have a firm vision of what your merchandise will look like and what financial decisions you need to make.

Too many new vendors fail because of poor planning. More often than not, they didn't do any research to find out what convention customers want or they don't understand how to make profitable business decisions about what merchandise to purchase. You, however, are on a different path. All the work you've done already has prepared you to avoid their mistakes.

To finalize your start-up plan, there are just two more assignments to go:

- Craft your merchandise plan.
- Create your business battle plan.

If you're in need of a can of Red Bull, grab it. These assignments need your full attention. Let's begin.

ASSIGNMENT #11:
Craft your merchandise plan

By this stage, the floodgates are open and ideas about what you want to include in your merchandise mix are pouring out. You know what categories are consistent sellers and you know which series are popular.

It's important to draft your merchandise plan now so that you can focus your product searches and purchases on a manageable number of items. It's easy to get distracted by shiny new things or new anime series – your merchandise plan gently smacks you upside your head to keep you focused on what works.

It's time to finalize the list of anime series you will stock and the merchandise items you will carry for each as you start up your vendor business.

STEP-BY-STEP INSTRUCTIONS:

1. Revisit your practice spreadsheet of your desired products. It's time to move from practice to the real deal. Go back and conduct product searches for all the anime on your 'investigate further' list.

   Your spreadsheet should include columns for:

   - The item description.
   - Item URL.
   - Item price or the auction's current bid (if applicable).
   - Auction ending date (if applicable).
   - The price you're willing to pay.
   - The proxy service fees and your estimated international shipping cost for each item.
   - Convention price.
   - Gross profit – convention price minus purchase price (including all fees and shipping cost).
   - Mark-up percentage (any item with at least a 100% mark-up stays on the list and any item with less is crossed off.)

2. Goup the items by anime.

3. Prioritize the anime on your list. Whichever anime has the most merchandise available with the highest gross profit gets skipped to the front of the line.

You may have your heart set on a massive display of *Sailor Moon* figures, but be open to letting the merchandise that's available lead you in another direction. Remember to target unique and exclusive items. These will give you a leg-up over other vendors.

If the majority of your merchandise falls in the minor product difference group, you'll have the least price flexibility. You'll have to stick close to what your competitors are charging. Get more flexibility by loading up your plan with products that are different from the standard stuff that lazier vendors are selling. You'll be able to charge a premium price for this merchandise.

Sensei tip: The sexy 'bad' boy, demon or animal merchandise is very popular with customers. But, contrary to popular belief, the good guys don't finish last. They'll match their bad boy brethren in sales as long as they have crazy-strong powers and occasionally cross over to the dark side.

Plan to have at least one eye-catching, heart-stopping item that attendees can spot from the aisle. Market-savvy vendors will always purchase one or two of these. They also usually have at least one supersize item that can be spotted from one hundred feet away for the same reason. This is a clever strategy to draw attention to your booth and entice customers to come in and look around. The items can be from any category or anime and not necessarily the ones you're focusing on.

For example, one comic book vendor carries *Yamashita* schoolgirl figures. Attendees walking down the aisle will always point and stare and then walk into his booth. These figures are very detailed, beautiful and expensive. They're priced at $150 or higher and are items most attendees wish they could afford. Convention-goers who may not normally stop are drawn to his booth to check out these figures (and hopefully see something else of interest that they can afford).

SELLING TO HEROES, VILLAINS AND GEEKS

> **Sensei tip:** Pause before stocking up on US merchandise from Warner Bros. or Disney (Marvel) franchises. Customers can purchase this type of merchandise from an endless number of US stores and vendors. They want something a little more adventurous and unique at cons.
>
> I've included a list of my favorite suppliers in the *Appendix* of this book if you need some help finishing your list.

When you are thinking about your merchandise strategy, I really want you to wake up screaming, 'It's not what I like; it's what the customers like!' Tattoo this on your brain and refer to it often.

My rookie vendor friends often don't understand my merchandising decisions because the items I stock are not something *they like* or something *they would buy*. Until they see me sell out, when all of a sudden those items don't seem so ridiculous anymore. They're still learning that a merchandise plan isn't something you should set in stone. And it definitely shouldn't be informed by your own tastes.

The good news is that all of the hard work has now been completed (yeah!). All you have to do now is write it all down in your business battle plan – the road map you will use to steer your vending decisions.

ASSIGNMENT #12:
Create your business battle plan

Your battle plan doesn't have to be long, just a few pages will do, but the benefits will be immeasurable. This is how it will help you:

- You'll stay on strategy. It's hard enough to stick to a strategy during your weekly routine of traveling to conventions and ordering merchandise, and particularly so if you don't document it and refer to it regularly.

- Your business objectives will be clear. Your plan will define specific measurable objectives and this will help you to achieve them.

- Your educated guesses will be better. Your plan informs and refines any guesswork you have to make about merchandise, pricing and customer targets.

- You can better manage your cash flow. No business can afford to mismanage its cash. And simple profits are rarely the same as cash when inventory ties up most of your money. Your plan helps you make business-savvy decisions that keep expenses low and profits high.

- Having a business plan gives you a way to be proactive – not reactive – in your business. Course corrections can save your business from flopping. Don't wait for things to happen (for example, an anime's popularity waning), plan for them. Follow up on changing trends by tracking your sales results, have new anime already researched and included on your spreadsheet as your backup plan, and make course corrections when warranted.

It's a myth that a business plan is supposed to predict the future. Instead, it sets out expectations and makes informed assumptions so that you can manage the future by correcting your course when needed. However, if your plan doesn't have any measurable objectives, it's not worth the paper it's written on. Your plan's sole purpose is to help you achieve your business goals. It helps clarify what you hope to achieve in your business and provides a basis for the decisions you'll make along the way. New vendors often fail to make course corrections because they don't have a back-up plan in place if they fail to meet their sales goals.

The good news is you don't need a big formal business plan to seize these benefits. Instead, think of your business plan as a collection of lists, bullet points and spreadsheets. It needs to be just big enough to do its job, so keep this in mind as you work your way through the final assignment. And while you're marking down your answers in this assignment, make darn sure you've thought through every question completely. For the sake of comparison, I've included my own business objectives and answers to the more general questions so you will have a working example to refer to.

STEP-BY-STEP INSTRUCTIONS:

1. Set your sales objective.

    The larger the dollar value in sales you hope to achieve, the more conventions you will need to attend. Keep this in mind when you set your objectives here. If you're planning for six figure sales then be prepared to spend the majority of the year traveling to thirty-five or forty conventions. In your first year, set a more manageable number to allow yourself the time to learn what works and what doesn't. Every show is different and your sales will hinge on your merchandise, the fans' budgets, the length of the convention, the number of vendors and the turnout. Your sales goal for your first few conventions should allow you to cover that show's expenses and the expenses for your next convention, at a bare minimum.

    Question: What is your sales objective? What time frame do you want to achieve this in?

    Your answer: My vendor business will generate X dollars over the next twelve months. (Fill in the dollar amount.)

2. Determine your sales channels.

    Your strategy may focus solely on conventions. The benefit of conventions is that they do all the work and bring customers to you.

    Perhaps you will also pursue selling items online. Or something more ambitious like opening a brick and mortar store or creating your own event. But, please, not in your first year. Keep in mind that each additional sales channel you include will require more time and money, along with a separate marketing plan to drive people to your store, website or event.

Question: Where do you plan to sell your merchandise?

Your answer: My merchandise will be sold at conventions and (fill in the blank if relevant). Be specific about which type of convention you'll target during your first year.

Author example: My merchandise will be sold at anime, comic, sci-fi, horror, paranormal and magic conventions. I will avoid comic book memorabilia shows or any convention that does not target anime fans. Convention attendance should exceed 2,000. Larger conventions (10,000+ attendees) within a 700-mile radius will take priority over smaller ones. I'll only vend at conventions lasting two or more days and will avoid all college-campus-hosted cons.

3. Nail down your target market and customer segments.

   If you are clear about the customers you are targeting, you'll be better positioned to give them what they want. The more you know and understand anime, comic, sci-fi, horror and paranormal fans, the better the purchasing decisions you'll make. You'll know which products are appealing and which ones don't merit further investigation. Be careful about targeting a limited pool of people by only carrying a specialized product line.

   Question: Who are your target customers?

   Your answer: My target customers are (fill in the blank). Include the genres or activities they are interested in.

   Author example: My target customers are anime fans who attend anime, comic, sci-fi, horror and paranormal conventions. Avid fans who are sixteen years and older and who love classic and popular manga/anime originating in Japan are my primary target.

4. Decide on what merchandise you will sell.

   Prioritize stocking your booth with exclusive anime or manga items that other vendors neglect to carry. Every aisle in a dealer room resembles a red carpet rolled out for the customers and it is vendors, not swarming paparazzi, that are eager to get their attention. The sure-fire way to get attendees to look in your direction and then magnetically pull them to your booth is the exclusive, unique or cutting-edge merchandise on display. You'll also want to fill any anime and merchandise category vacancies left unattended by other vendors.

Question: What type of merchandise do you plan to sell?

Your answer: My merchandise will be a mix of (fill in the blank).

Try to include a mix of merchandise with a combination of the three product difference classifications.

Author example: My primary merchandising strategy centers on anime plushies, with a heavy emphasis on Pokémon. I aim to offer the largest selection and sizes of exclusive Japanese-distributed Pokémon plushies and characters compared to any other vendor.

I'll also feature merchandise from other classic anime shows (for example, Black Butler, Dragon Ball and Fullmetal Alchemist) to fill niches and add variety. I'll offer several popular items (plushies, figures, pocket watches, necklaces, rings and key chains) for each anime I stock.

I'll also temporarily rotate in merchandise from one of the latest anime shows with at least one TV season under its belt. I'll ride the wave of its popularity until the Chinese wholesalers catch up with their bootleg versions or otherwise unique and exclusive merchandise becomes harder and harder to find at bargain prices.

Finally, I'll aim to opportunistically purchase several premium-priced, eye-popping, heart-stopping items that grab the attention of attendees. These items will be unique merchandise that is only sold in Japan.

 Sensei tip: My absolute favorite items to sell and that I LOVE more than life itself are ... any items the customers rush to buy!

5. Set your convention prices.

   Decide if most of your merchandise will be priced in a low price range (less than $10), a medium price range ($10 - $50), or a high price range ($50 or more).

Your pricing will depend on your products and the prices at which you purchase them. The exclusivity and uniqueness of your items should be factored into the price, but don't expect customers to pay big bucks if the perceived value isn't there.

Question: What is your pricing strategy?

Your answer: My merchandise will be priced between X and Y dollars. (Fill in your estimated price range.)

Author example: The majority of merchandise will be priced between $20 and $50. A second category of items priced between $5 and $14 will also be available, depending on favorable acquisition prices. Items priced over $50 will be obtained in small quantities to meet the eye-popping, heart-stopping merchandise objective. All convention prices are based on a minimum 100% mark-up but most prices will be closer to a 200% mark-up target.

> **Sensei tip**: Can't figure out the right price for an item? Google search the item and see who's selling it at what price. I frequently do this to make sure the item I'm purchasing hasn't made it to the US market. Or, if it has, what's the retail price?

6. Figure out your budget and identify a funding source.

   Acquiring your inventory and paying vendor fees adds up quickly before you even make one sale. If you're starting from a base of zero, you'll have to allocate several hundred dollars for purchasing inventory. Once you add in shipping costs, the initial investment will likely be over one thousand dollars. This inventory should carry you through two or three conventions, but there are other costs you need to budget for too:

   - Vendor fees. These can be as low as $200 but are more likely to approach $400 for each convention. Also, if vendor spots are in high demand, you'll have to book and pay for several cons months in advance to secure your booth. It's not unheard of to have to pay for a popular convention nine months in advance.

- Booth display supplies. These can be minimal at first, but eventually you'll spend another couple of hundred dollars to properly display your merchandise.
- Other expenses incurred for each convention include gas, parking, food and hotel costs for out-of-town shows.

Once you begin to generate sales, you will be able to offset some of these costs. But because you're in startup mode, initial profits will need to be reinvested into inventory and vendor fees for upcoming shows.

Question: What is your budget? How much can you invest in inventory?

Your answer: My initial dollar investment will be X dollars. (Fill in the amount you are able to invest up front.)

Based on this answer, you should revisit your merchandise plan and decide how many items on your spreadsheet you'll be able to purchase.

Once you have answered these questions, you will have laid out your basic business strategy. You are very clear about your direction and the decisions that work best for your business. Your battle plan is ready for launch!

So, what's next? Are you pumped to register for your first convention? Since all conventions are not created equal, the next chapter gives you the lowdown on how to weed out the good conventions from the bad ones. It's time to initiate your launch sequence.

PART 3:

INITIATE LAUNCH SEQUENCE

No more excuses. It's time to find some conventions to sign up for and start vending. Your city or state may or may not be overflowing with conventions. But hopefully there is a convention within a 300-mile radius. Road trip! And since all conventions don't have the same sales potential, we'll discuss a few things for your selection thought process that are more sophisticated than eenie meenie miney mo.

Also, once you've registered for your first convention, there is still a heap of important things to do so that you are super prepared. We are going to cover logistics, checklists, small details that make a big difference and your booth setup to get you prepped and ready-to-go. Then we'll talk customer service, walk through a day-by-day breakdown of vendor activities during a convention, and put a glaring spotlight on the financial truths you need to be aware of.

Don't skip over this bit; it's the third act!

CONVENTION ROAD MAP

TO GET STARTED, YOU NEED to find the right convention for your launch into vending. Visit **upcomingcons.com** for a list of conventions in your area.

Another way to find out about conventions is to talk to other vendors about upcoming shows they're planning on attending. If they have invested in vendor fees, they must think the show is a good one. Just be mindful that asking other vendors about whether to attend a convention or not can be dicey. Their prior history with that show or its staff may bias their response. On the other hand, if vendors say the convention was a ghost town (meaning low attendance) and most vendors left early, then listen.

 Sensei tip: Vendors lie. Their 'bad report' about a convention could be because their merchandise stunk up the joint and have nothing to do with the convention itself. On the other hand, I've also heard some vendors rave about how wonderful their sales were when the convention was a graveyard, all the vendors left early and the convention shut its doors for good. The bottom line is: Only ask vendors you really trust to give you an objective answer.

Once you've done a bit of research and put together a list of potential conventions, you need to narrow down your options. I'll point out a few things that can help you to find the conventions that are worth pursuing.

Consider your merchandise

Does the 'convention theme + your merchandise = perfect match'?

Select conventions where the theme is related to the type of merchandise you are going to sell. We have spoken about this a little already. Remember the comic book memorabilia show and the vendor with the chess and magic card sets? His result: No sales. Or, the chair massage vendor at a horror convention. His result: No sales. I just can't emphasize enough how important it is to make sure your merchandise fits with the interests of the con attendees.

Your merchandise and customer targets should determine the types of convention to attend. I keep getting invited to a *My Little Pony* convention by a slightly desperate vendor-room coordinator. But their fan base – kids under twelve years old – is not one of my customer targets. Plus I don't sell any My Little Pony merchandise. It's not part of my business battle plan, so it's not a convention I would consider.

> **Oops alert:** I once went to a convention that covered sci-fi, science, horror movies, comics, toys, video gaming, TV, films, anime, manga, wrestling, MMA, original art, paranormal and collectibles – wow, that's a mouthful! But sixty percent of the vendors didn't sell merchandise related to *any* of these themes. Wind chimes with flowers ... really? And these vendors were pissed because they didn't sell one item during the two-day convention. They vowed not to come back (and obviously, they shouldn't).

It's not the convention's fault if you don't do your homework and end up at the wrong convention with unpopular merchandise.

Size does matter

Imagine this: 133,000 people, 1,855 panels and events, 765 vendors and 206 artists. These numbers are estimates from San Diego Comic Con International – the biggest North American pop culture convention. Impressive, right? But my advice to you as a vendor is that your first few conventions should be a wee bit smaller than this.

Depending on what conventions are in your area, you'll want to try and launch your vendor business at a show with about 2,000 attendees. Don't immediately jump in the deep end with a large three-day convention and 15,000+ attendees to deal with. Large shows require a much higher inventory investment to meet your sales projections based on the attendance numbers.

When you are starting out, you won't have a clue about what your bestsellers will be. Thus, the financially-prudent approach is to only invest in enough inventory to carry you through a few small shows.

Starting smallish allows you time to observe which items are selling well from your own stock as well as at other booths. Just be aware that if the show is too small (less than 600 attendees), you won't get a good sense of what sells. Six hundred might sound large, but over three days, all this results in is twenty vendors spending too much time twiddling their thumbs. Based on the categorizations below, you'll want to start out on the lower end of medium size shows.

Convention sizes	Attendance
Small	<1,000
Medium	1,001 – 7,500
Large	7,501 – 25,000
Mega	25,001 – 150,000

Set a sales goal for each convention you attend based on the expected attendance. While large conventions happily shout record-breaking attendance numbers on their website, you'll have to hunt for the attendance figures of the smaller conventions.

To get an idea of numbers, start your search on the convention's website and Facebook page. No luck there? Try a Google search with the convention's name and the words 'attendance figures.' If a Wikipedia answer pops up, click on the link. There will often be an event history sub-heading where you can find the annual attendance figures. For example, enter **en.wikipedia.org/wiki/Anime_Central** in your browser. Look for the event history heading and you'll see a table with Anime Central's estimated annual attendance numbers.

Of course, you can always email the vendor room coordinator and ask how many people they expect to attend. Just remember that they want to sell you a booth, so greet their answer with a hefty dose of skepticism.

Does the convention make the cut?

When you're starting out, you'll often need to rely on your best judgment about which convention to register for based on the information at hand. However, let me give you a few tips to keep in mind.

As a general rule, avoid any first-year conventions held in hotels or on college campuses. These conventions haven't built a large fan base yet. You don't want vendors tossing a football in the aisles because they're bored (yes, this has happened). Having said this, I do have a friend that does really well at college campus conventions so these are a top priority for her. But for most vendors, it's small pickings.

The exception to this rule is first-year conventions held at exhibit halls in convention centers. Veteran promoters who know how to attract large crowds operate these shows. Even so, there is no guarantee people will actually show up for a first-year show. So, proceed with caution.

For example, one first-year show I attended was fabulous and attracted 11,000 attendees. The convention was held in a location that had very few entertainment alternatives. It was a hit! My booth had record sales. But at another first-year show, held in a city oversaturated with conventions, my booth sales hit a record low. The show attracted very few fans and the first year was also its last year.

Your safest bet is to register for conventions that have at least a three-year history. First, these conventions are better organized. Second, they have proven themselves as legit. And finally, these conventions should attract at least 1,000 attendees. You can find a convention's birth year by visiting its website. It'll be in the 'FAQs' or 'About us' section.

> **Oops alert:** I signed up for a convention that was in its third year. The promoter was established and operated several conventions annually. A few weeks before this convention, I still hadn't received all of the necessary vendor information and the staff weren't responding to my emails. This is never a good sign.

> So, I contacted a celebrity guest who I knew personally to confirm whether or not the convention was a 'go.' She said it was, so I went ahead and made the four-hour drive to attend it. The convention went on as scheduled, but it was disorganized and a disaster. Once the convention ended that year, it ended permanently.

Other factors that should be considered in your 'maybe yes, maybe no' deliberations are:

- Conventions in cities or states with only one or two shows scheduled each year are great. Fans are starving for this type of entertainment and the turnout will be big.

- Cities that have high disposable income are ideal because the fans have plenty of discretionary spending money.

- Multiple conventions concentrated in a small geographical area over a short period of time will dilute the fan base. Fans will target the larger conventions with the most activities and celebrity guests and pass on the medium and smaller ones.

- Be aware of all convention dates in your area. Large convention dates shift from one year to the next. The change in timing has the potential to crush another smaller convention in the area. This can cause a significant drop-off in attendance and a whole lot of bitchin' from the smaller show's organizer (and the vendors!).

- Skip conventions that are rumored to be poorly-run. They're not worth the aggravation they will give you. Both attendees and vendors end up griping and complaining about the disorganized chaos.

> **Sensei tip:** Every convention is a financial risk. As I explained to a new vendor who asked about a refund – the convention won't give refunds to vendors because attendance was dismal or the vendors didn't make any money.

> **Sensei tip:** Avoid convention advice from vendors who also run their own shows. It is against the laws of nature for them to say anything nice about someone else's convention. Unseemly as it is, show promoters are known to trash talk and spread rumors about other conventions, hoping they'll fail.

No room at the inn

In your search, you'll come across conventions where all of the vendor slots have already been filled. In this instance, the website will blare the message: 'VENDOR ROOM SOLD OUT.' If you have your heart set on being a vendor at one of these, look for instructions about reserving a spot on the waiting list.

The most popular big conventions sell out their vendor spots quickly and have an extensive waiting list. Years can pass before new vendors finally get off the waiting list and into the convention. Others may not even accept new vendors or limit the number of new vendor spots or may require references before approving you. Even getting into popular small and medium-size conventions can be tricky. The smaller vendor rooms can sell out in a blink of the eye.

But take heart. Plenty of popular conventions are open to first-time vendors. Just be sure to sign up as soon as vendor registration opens.

Sensei tip: To register for large and mega conventions before vendor space sells out, check their websites frequently. Registration for the next year's convention may open up shortly after the current convention ends.

Sensei tip: Check to see how many other vendors have signed up for a convention. Some convention websites list the number of vendors attending or the number of booths still available. If less than fifty percent of the spaces have been sold and the convention is right around the corner, then be very leery about why this is and do some further investigating.

Build your convention list

Okay – grab a calendar. Identify several conventions you'd like to attend over the next six months. Where possible, space your conventions far enough apart (two or three weeks) so that new inventory from overseas has time to arrive if you need it.

For your first convention, select one that averages 2,000 attendees. The dealer room will have a moderate pace that provides ample opportunity to observe customer reactions to your merchandise and their interactions with other vendors. I launched my vendor business at a one-day convention four hours from my house. Fifteen hundred people attended. By observing other vendors, I picked up several eye-opening tips (all of them revealed throughout this book) for my second convention outing. And your learning will go to a whole new level when you experience the 'sensei tips' and 'oops alerts' (revealed throughout this book) in action.

The road to vendor registration

As far as most conventions are concerned, it doesn't matter whether you're big or small, old or new, veteran or inexperienced. As long as there is space available and you can pay the vendor fee, you're good to go.

While a few conventions have a pre-approval process to help limit the number of vendors selling the same thing or use a jury process to pick and choose which vendors get approved, most conventions are first come, first served. If you do find a convention that has an approval process, you'll just have to submit the application and wait for further instructions.

The registration process can be completed in a few easy steps:

1. Locate the convention you want to register for.

2. You can go directly to the convention website if you know the URL or you can use **upcomingcons.com** to find it. The dates and locations for anime, comic and multi-genre conventions are all posted here. Another option is to visit **animecons.com** and click the convention tab for the dates and locations of anime conventions.

3. On the convention website, click on the **Vendor, Exhibitor or Dealer** tab. Again, for simplicity's sake, I use the word 'vendor' but it is interchangeable with exhibitor or dealer. Do not select the artist tab.

4. Follow the vendor registration instructions.

5. You will need to submit both your application details and payment for your booth. Conventions normally require full payment upfront to secure a spot.

Some conventions will have a short online form for registration and others will ask you to download a PDF file and fill it out manually. Applications can be brief, just two pages, or they can be a huge manifesto. In either case, you will need to provide your name, company name, address, contact information, description of the items you'll be selling, the number of booths desired, and so on.

 I've included an example of a vendor application form in the *Appendix* of this book so you can get an idea of what this looks like.

What you need to know

In one form or another, the convention will provide you with the following standard information:

- Booth size – The dimensions of the booth (typically 10' x 10').

- Booth location – At some conventions, you can select your location. A floor plan will be included in the application or in the vendor section of the website. But at others, the convention assigns them based on their criteria, which hitherto remains a complete mystery. If you have the option to select your booth location, the spaces closest to the entrance are the most desirable spots.

- Booth prices – These are listed on a per booth basis. Inner booths (ones with vendors on either side of you) are cheaper than corner booths.

- Items included with each booth – Usually, a table, tablecloth, two chairs, two vendor badges and a company sign are part of the price.

- Dealer-room hours – The hours the dealer room will be open for business.

- Load-in hours – The time vendors can begin setting up their booths. Setup occurs the day before the convention and the morning of the first day, but sometimes load-in occurs only on the morning of the first day. Some conventions even pre-assign load-in hours for each vendor to prevent traffic jams at the loading dock. If the load-in hours are not in the application form, check the website. If no load-in hours are listed, the convention will send an email shortly before the event with the information. On the second and subsequent days of the con, vendors can access the dealer room at least one hour prior to opening.

- Load-out hours – Dismantling your booth happens at the end of the convention. The show's organizers warn dealers not to break down before closing time or they'll face the wrath of the convention gods.

- Convention rules – For example, no tacking anything on the walls *ever*.

- Cancellation policy – This will detail the deadlines and the amount of any refund. It will be clearly spelled out in the application.

- Convention staff and relevant contact information.

- Registration details – Where and how to submit the application along with the accepted forms of payment (for example: Online shopping cart, check, credit card or PayPal).

Other information might also be provided, such as the location of the dealer room inside the hotel or convention center, electricity and Wi-Fi information, and parking facilities and fees. Any additional details and reminders will be emailed to you closer to the convention date. And you can always contact the dealer-room coordinator for more information if you need it.

Convention attendance from year to year can be erratic for no apparent reason. Larger, established conventions tend to be more stable than medium or smaller ones. It's the nature of the business. Now, with the convention and vendor registration road maps fresh in your mind, we'll move on to prepping for your first convention. You are officially open for business (imaginary high five).

CONVENTION LOGBOOK

THIS CHAPTER RUNS THROUGH SOME logistics, checklists and last-minute details that must be sorted out as you prepare for your first convention. This will help you avoid any last-minute, ugly surprises.

The 'L' Word

Yes, it's time to review the dreaded logistics to guarantee a smooth and successful vendor outing. You don't want to give yourself heart palpitations at your very first convention because a few small, but important, details slipped through the cracks. They're fairly basic, so we'll fast-forward through these to make sure you are fully prepped for your business launch.

You'll need to think about storage, transportation, payment methods, state business registration and even sales tax before you turn up ready to vend. So let's get to it!

Storage wars

Whose stuff are you getting rid of to make room for your inventory? Or are you planning on negotiating an obstacle course of boxes every time you want to get from your living room to the kitchen?

Plan to solve your storage space conundrum prior to the arrival of your first shipment of merchandise. The ideal space will meet these requirements:

- Provides easy access.
- Is big enough to allow you to search through, sort and group items.

- Protects and keeps your inventory in excellent condition.
- Can fit both your booth display supplies and inventory.

If where you live doesn't have that kind of space, it may be time for a yard sale or you might consider renting a storage shed or unit.

In addition to storage space, ideally, you'll want to carve out a workspace (perhaps your dining room table?). When your shipments arrive, you have to inspect them, make sure every item is accounted for, put sticker prices on them and make sure there are no quality issues.

Occasionally, newly-arrived items need minor repairs. DIY was never my specialty but I can change a watch battery. If you sell plushies, watches (or anything with a battery), you'll need a few inexpensive items:

- Travel-size sewing needles, thread and Liquid Fusion clear glue. If a piece of material becomes unglued or stitches unravel, you can quickly repair the item.
- Cell batteries. For the cheapest prices, search eBay.
- Mini eyeglass screwdriver to open battery compartments. The screwdriver needs to have both a flat and a Phillips head.
- Impulse Sealer (American International Electric Inc.) and polypropylene (transparent) bags. This equipment heat-seals bags closed in half a second. Placing items in a bag keeps them pristine and clean from dust and fingerprints. The heat-sealed bag also makes your merchandise look more retail ready. Search eBay for cellophane bags or visit **clearbags.com for polypropylene ones.**

 Sensei tip: Instead of leaving small items loose, also place them in a bag. If a customer is thinking about purchasing an item, they don't like to see it unprotected while being manhandled by a bunch of other folk. They'll place a higher value on merchandise *sealed* (not taped) inside a bag.

Make sure you have adequate space available to store and prepare your merchandise. As you unpack from one convention, you'll probably be repacking for the next one; the more space you have to maneuver, the quicker you can complete this task.

Transportation

Of course, you'll also need to be able to transport all that merchandise and your display supplies to the convention as well. So, both your inventory and your supplies must fit into your vehicle. And don't forget, it will have to hold three days' worth of inventory for out-of-town conventions.

If your vehicle doesn't have the required space, you may need to consider renting a U-Haul van. For conventions close to home, this is fine, but when traveling long distances, the mileage fee will drain your profit (it's approximately $0.59/mile). Therefore, this mode of transportation won't be financially feasible.

I manage to fit all of my supplies and inventory for a three-day convention into my 2000 two-door Honda Accord. Yes, you read that correctly! Of course, my items fill every nook and cranny, plus I pack the trunk to the brim. Heck, who needs to see out the back window anyway?

As my business has grown, I have added a U-Haul hitch to the back of my car out of necessity. Renting a five by eight foot trailer costs less than $20 a day and doesn't have any mileage fees.

There are a few drawbacks to using the trailer. You have to be able to hitch and unhitch it from your car. This requires a certain amount of strength and it helps if you can bench press fifty pounds! Also, parking the trailer takes some forethought. It will occupy three parking spaces and the parking lots at hotel conventions can be full of guest cars. You'll need plenty of room to maneuver the trailer, unhitch it and park it in a separate space.

Sensei tip: If you rent a trailer, *buy* those plastic wheel chocks for $10.99. They keep the trailer from hurtling out of control if you park and unhitch it on a slightly elevated surface. And trust me, minor elevations are problematic. Even when you're inside loading or unloading inventory, the unhitched trailer can easily move back and forth if it's not on an absolutely flat surface.

Pulling a trailer also wreaks havoc on your gas mileage. You can expect fuel costs to increase by about one-third. Plus, constantly pulling a trailer strains your car's engine. So, I recommend only using this option for large out-of-town conventions that are more than several hours away.

Make sure you include regular car maintenance in your budget. You don't want to be stranded on the side of the road with a carload of inventory, six hours from home.

Cash, credit or debit?

Most attendees will pay cash at conventions, so you need to be prepared to make change from larger bills. Start off the convention with at least $200 in change made up of $1, $5 and $10 bills.

If you are going to accept credit or debit card purchases, I recommend the credit processing service Square (squareup.com). Square works with iPhone, iPad and Android devices and it accepts Visa, MasterCard, Discover and American Express. Their newest credit card reader also works with both magnetic strip and the new EMV (Europay, MasterCard, Visa) credit cards that are equipped with computer chips that authenticate the chip-card transaction.

The main features of Square are:

- It accepts and archives credit card payments.
- It tracks sales.
- It allows you to create an item library with names, prices, images and descriptions.
- It records full or partial refunds.
- It issues digital receipts.
- It compiles daily summary reports.

Square allows you to enter each price manually on your device at the time of the transaction. Or, to keep your transactions moving speedily along, create a library of your items and preload the prices. Then you simply have to select the item being purchased and the total amount automatically reflects the price. Square will not accept or process any credit transactions that are rejected by the credit card holder's issuing bank. While you won't be asked to cut up their credit card, a message will appear on your screen saying the card has been declined.

For each transaction, Square offers two options for receipts. Buyers can either enter their text number or email address for an immediate record of their purchase. There is also a 'no thank you' option for customers who decline a receipt. Square will email you a copy of the receipt whether or not the customer chooses to receive one. If you have preloaded the item price and description, this information is included on the receipt. In the case of a credit card dispute, this makes it easy for you to tell exactly what the customer purchased.

Customer payments are first sent to Square, which deducts its fee. This is a percentage of the sales price. Square then forwards the remaining funds directly to your bank account. Deposits generally occur within forty-eight hours of the transaction. Oh yeah, using Square also hits your telephone's data plan so be aware of that.

Sensei tip: Purchase the inexpensive stylus pen for your smartphone. This makes it much easier for customers to sign the credit card authorization on your touch screen than using their finger to write their signature.

Of course, if this sounds like too much hassle, you can always decide to only accept cash. But some attendees don't carry cash. Or the onsite ATM runs out of cash. Or customers spend more than they anticipated and want to charge their remaining purchases. Approximately thirty-five percent of my customers use their credit card to pay for purchases. Also, every customer spending over one hundred dollars wants to pay with a credit card. With the introduction of Square, accepting credit cards is a no-brainer. And if it means more sales ... why not?

Oops alert: A vendor selling expensive collectible toys decided 'cash only' was going to be his policy at the beginning of a large convention. On Friday, the second day of the convention, he realized he was losing several hundred dollars in daily sales by only accepting cash. The onsite ATMs, as usual, quickly ran out of money. After thinking about his 'cash only' policy overnight, he decided accepting credit cards was a more prudent course of action. But, what about customers who wanted to use their credit cards on Saturday, the largest day of the convention? You can't get the Square credit card reader in a few hours. His solution was to ask me (his booth neighbor)

> **!** to charge his customer's credit card to my account and then to give him the cash. Really?! I agreed but I don't recommend you try this approach. Think about your customers – and your vendor colleagues – and make life easy for them by setting up an account with a secure credit card processing service ahead of time.

State business registration

States mandate that any business conducting transactions must be registered with the state and collect and pay sales tax. Your business must be registered in your home state and each state where your vendor business travels. I want to give you a heads-up here – a few vendor applications will ask for a (state or Federal) tax identification number.

Acquiring your state tax ID number is a two-step online process. Step one is to register with your home state and pay the applicable fee. After receiving confirmation and approval from the state, you can then complete step two and register with the Department of Revenue to obtain your state tax identification number. If you are registering for an out-of-state convention, after you've completed these two steps in your home state, you also repeat these steps for the state of the out-of-state convention. You'll then have your state's tax ID number and a separate tax ID number from the state where the convention is being held. When registering your business in a state - other than your home state -, you'll need to sign up with a registered agent located in the state of the convention. States require a mailing address within the state to receive tax information. Registered agents, for an annual fee, will act as your mail and email forwarding service.

Read the vendor application *very carefully*. It may contain information on additional licenses required by the county, city or state of the convention.

Okay, that was the thirty-second, bird's eye view of the state registration process. And I haven't covered federal registration or sales tax reporting and payment. This is your responsibility as a business owner.

The ball is one hundred percent in your court to follow all federal and state laws, and seek professional legal and financial advice.

Convention prices and the state sales tax

There are two ways you can handle collecting sales tax on each purchase, assuming you are registered with the state of the convention. You've seen retail prices with the 'sales tax not included' statement and this is one option. Otherwise, you can include the tax in the price.

For example, let's say you charge $20 for a pocket watch. Look at the effect of sales tax on the final price in the following two scenarios:

Scenario 1 – Sales tax included in price

Money collected from buyer	$20.00
Actual price of item	$18.69
State sales tax (7%)	$1.31

Scenario 2 – Sales tax added to price

Money collected from buyer	$21.40
Price of item	$20.00
State sales tax (7%)	$1.40

How you handle sales tax is entirely up to you. I have made my decision based on the pros and cons of each scenario. So let's run through a few of these now so you can decide what's best for you. The pros for including sales tax in the price (scenario 1) are:

- Speed and convenience. Your booth may become extremely busy. You won't have to calculate the sales tax for every price point and count out coins for every transaction.

- Not dealing with coins means less hassle for both you and your customers. Jangling coins are not a welcome accessory for cosplay outfits.

- Customers can quickly figure out the total amount owed. An item priced for $5 sells for $5. Customers know to pull out a $5 bill and not $5.35 (the price with 7% tax added).

- When customers ask, 'What about the sales tax?' I get to say that it's included in the price. A look of relief comes over their face and they feel like they're getting an even better bargain.

- Some customers might remark, 'I only have $40.' This type of statement (with various whole dollar amounts) is repeated numerous times and especially on Sundays. If the customer wants to purchase two items priced for $20 each, then they know they owe you $40 and not $42.80 (the price with 7% tax added), which is $2.80 more than they can afford.

I've never worried about going any further with my list of pros and cons for either scenario because of that last point. Customers just don't take into account tax when they're trying to spend their last few dollars. I want to make it as easy as possible for them to empty their wallet at my booth. Including the sales tax in the price keeps life simple for customers and vendors.

Pre-convention planning dispatch checklist

The date has finally arrived for your first convention. You've organized everything and vendor load-in starts tomorrow. You're going to need a good night's sleep. This is your twenty-four-hour countdown. This is my motto:

> 'The best preparation for tomorrow is to do today's work superbly well.'
> – William Osler

If you've ever moved from one location to another, you know the headache of packing everything and taking care of a thousand minor details. Well, packing for a convention entails the same kind of effort. And once you arrive at a convention, especially a non-local one, you can't turn around and run home to grab the stuff you forgot. So you're left with stalking other vendors, hoping they have what you need.

Before you put the key in the ignition and peel out of your parking space, make sure you have everything on this checklist!

- Directions to the convention site.
- Copy of your completed vendor application.
- Copy of your vendor confirmation email.
- State Sales Tax certificate or authorization.

- Fully charged iPhone or Android device.
- Cash – $200 in $1, $5 and $10 bills.
- Display supplies.
- Hand truck – Superman is usually not available, so you need a way to transport your inventory from your vehicle to the dealer room.
- Merchandise – A few days before the convention, organize your merchandise to make unloading and setup easy.
- Pack your vendor go bag, which contains a host of must-have items, including:

  - ☑ Scissors
  - ☑ Tape
  - ☑ Phone charger
  - ☑ Advil
  - ☑ Fingernail clipper
  - ☑ Hand lotion
  - ☑ Extra pre-priced labels
  - ☑ Business cards
  - ☑ Thank you bags
  - ☑ Tissues
  - ☑ Pen, marker
  - ☑ Band-Aids
  - ☑ Water
  - ☑ Garbage bags
  - ☑ Square credit card reader
  - ☑ Tablecloth or tarps to cover your booth overnight
  - ☑ Flashlight
  - ☑ Counterfeit bill detector pen
  - ☑ A long-sleeve shirt – The air conditioner will be set to full blast in hotel ballrooms and convention halls during the summer, resulting in subzero temperatures.

Always complete one last *extra* walkthrough to make sure your merchandise and supplies are fully loaded.

> **Oops alert:** At a mega convention, my booth neighbor went to the Miami Beach Convention Center to set up. Unfortunately, the convention's location was the Miami *Airport* Convention Center. They arrived at the correct location five minutes before the dealer room opened and were utterly stressed out – details count!

Last minute, nitty-gritty details

Sorting out the nitty-gritty details will include checking the obvious stuff as well as being aware of any last-minute changes made by the convention. Let's go through a few things that can catch you unaware.

Confirm that the convention's website lists your name or company as a participating vendor.

Oops alert: During vendor load-in, an out-of-town vendor discovered their name wasn't on the list even though they had paid and submitted an application form. Uh-oh! The vendor had to find the right person to talk to (good luck with that) to try and get the problem fixed. And, this long delay cut into their setup time. I believe they eventually got a booth (vendor spots were completely sold out), but I didn't see them again, so who knows? Murphy's Law is always in effect.

The day before the convention, re-check the dealer-room hours posted on the website. Frequently, the hours of operation listed on the application don't match the hours posted on the website or in the printed program. Whatever is printed in the souvenir program, even if it's a misprint, will be the official hours of operation.

Have I mentioned you should pack a boatload of patience? It will frequently be tested. I recall a two-day convention where load-in was scheduled for 6 am on the first day of the convention. However, the day before the convention, the website listed a new load-in time of 5 am. A few vendors arrived to unload at that *very early* hour but the security guard denied them access to the dealer room. The guard's schedule said load-in was at 6:30 am. The guard spoke to his boss who said vendors should *not* be granted access to the building. What the #$@&%*?! It's 5 am in the morning, dark and we're freezing our butts off standing outside.

One vendor called the show promoter, who arrived ten minutes later. After a heated phone conversation between the promoter and the security boss, the promoter agreed to pay the security firm for the one and a half hours of earlier load-in time. Finally, at 5:45 am, vendors were able to unload their stuff.

Plan to arrive early on the first day of load-in, especially if booth locations are assigned on the morning of the convention. This was the case in the 5 am example. I was one of those who arrived early and it benefited me in two ways:

1. I asked for a better and larger booth spot and that is what I got. Hey, did I mention I arrived at 5 am based on their website information and *before* the show promoter or their staff? The promoter felt bad about the 'tense' scene with security that was witnessed by a few vendors and made up for it by letting us choose our booth locations.

2. I didn't have to wait in line to unload. The limited loading-dock parking spaces filled up quickly. Vendors who arrived at 5 am claimed the open spots and avoided having to wait in line while other vendors unloaded.

I'm always surprised by the small size of loading-docks. Time and time again, vendors wait for space (the wait can exceed an hour) to free up before they can begin unloading. Get there early to avoid the wait.

Once inside the dealer room, you'll be dodging the boxes of other vendors while carting in your own stuff. Vendors, myself included, take every inch of assigned booth space and whatever else we can get away with. On occasion, the measuring tape has been known to pop out and resolve arguments over where one booth ends and another begins. Pack a friendly smile along with your measuring tape!

 Sensei tip: Like movie theatres, convention centers don't allow outside food or drink to be brought in. Bring your snacks inside during load-in unless you want to pay $10 for a hamburger. Once the convention opens, security checks the bags of everyone entering the building.

And one last tidbit: Stress levels tend to rise for everyone during load-in and setup. However, no matter the problem, patience resolves most things. Make sure you get yourself in the zone before arriving at the convention.

In this chapter, I've tried to lessen the fear of the unknown for you. Arriving at your first convention can be daunting, but if you're well-prepared, you'll manage just fine and will become a veteran before you know it.

The next stage of the vending start-up process involves designing a booth display that places each item in the customer's line of sight. Can you bench press fifty pounds? Is Superman a good friend of yours? The purpose of these questions becomes very clear in the next chapter.

WHERE'S SUPERMAN WHEN YOU NEED HIM?

F**ASTER THAN A SPEEDING BULLET!** More powerful than a locomotive! Able to leap tall buildings at a single bound! No, it's not Superman – it's just the vendors unloading their stuff and tirelessly setting up their booths.

Safety alert: Unloading and setting up is hard work. Make sure you put safety first – lift with your legs, not with your back – and pack some Advil.

Take a tour of any vendor room and you'll notice vendors with shelving, gridwall panels and extra tables to display as much merchandise as they possibly can. Pay attention to which items have been placed at eye-level, elevated, clamped on drapes or displayed on racks. While you're standing smack-dab in the middle of the aisle, observe whether customers are adequately able to see all the items, touch them and freely move around the booth. Make a mental note of what works and what doesn't.

Booth setups

It's your booth. You can do whatever you like. Experienced vendors know how to cram a tremendous amount of inventory into a small space so that they can save on booth fees. They also use height to their advantage by stacking items on shelves and building displays ten feet tall or higher. You want attendees to have a clear line of sight to everything you have for sale. People can't buy what they can't see.

At convention halls, booths are traditionally surrounded by pipe and drapes. Hotel ballrooms, on the other hand, place vendor tables just a few feet apart with no clear line of demarcation. Booth sizes vary but the three most common ones are 10' x 10', 8' x 10' and 8' x 8'.

Each space includes a table, tablecloth and two chairs. When you first walk into the convention hall to begin setting up your booth, the room will be set up with the table flush against the aisle.

Arriving vendors immediately change the setup within their allotted space so they can erect their displays. For example, I immediately move the table to the back of the booth and add two additional tables and one bench to create more surface area for my merchandise. This personalized setup triples my display space and allows people to walk into the booth. The walkway area provides a peaceful rest spot away from the crowded aisle. Customers can leisurely examine all of my merchandise.

If you keep the table pressed against the aisle in your layout, customers have to fight to maintain their shopping position or they'll be caught up in the flow of the crowd and swept right past your booth. At large conventions, don't underestimate how hard people have to fight to stop and look at your merchandise. During the busiest hours, aisles are jam-packed. People will be brushing against your customers while they are examining your merchandise. 'Sorry,' 'Excuse me,' and 'Pardon,' are very common refrains as people bang into each other. If you have any merchandise that customers will want to try on, you should create a secure space away from the crowded aisle. You want customers to linger at your booth and consider your items without the fear of bumps, bruises and public scrutiny.

At each convention, a slight change to your layout will be necessary depending on the actual size of your space, booth location, width of the aisle, the entrance and exit doors and, surprisingly, your neighbor's setup. If one neighbor erects a display wall eight feet high along the side where the booths connect but your other neighbor has no wall at all, you will probably need to adjust the placement of your items for the best exposure. Some neighbors will freely offer to let you hang items on the back of their display wall that faces into your booth.

Ninety-nine percent of your setup stays the same regardless of your neighbor's layout, but minor adjustments are always necessary. After a while they will become more intuitive.

Sensei tip: Be nice to your booth neighbor even if they're a little annoying during setup time. Vendors ask for little favors from each other all the time and you never know when you'll be the one doing the asking.

When planning your layout, an important consideration is whether you're flying solo or have worker bees to help you out. Flying solo means you can't purchase heavy supplies (anything weighing more than fifty pounds) or design a layout that requires more than one set of hands.

To determine the best design and necessary supplies, consider the following questions:

- Is your merchandise suited for tabletop display only?

- How much merchandise do you want to display? I'm always surprised when vendors (such as comic book publishers) only put a few items on a table. Will anybody even notice them?

- Do you need shelves or racks?

- Are there any hanging items? (For example, T-shirts, costumes or wall scrolls.)

- Do you need props to properly display items like hats or jewelry? (For example, mannequin heads or necklace stands.)

- Do you have any fragile items that will be displayed behind a glass case?

- Where are you going to keep extra inventory? (Hint: Hiding it underneath tables efficiently uses your booth space.)

- Do you want convention-goers to walk into your booth or only have access from the aisle?

- What about banners and signs? One Japanese snack vendor erected a huge thirty-foot sign that attendees could see from across the room – clever!

- How many booths per convention do you want to purchase on a regular basis?

SELLING TO HEROES, VILLAINS AND GEEKS

> **Sensei tip:** Customers want to hold items they are thinking about purchasing. They want to show them to their friends so, knowing this, most vendors place items within arm's reach of customers. *Let me repeat, people are much more likely to purchase an item if they can touch it.* I've witnessed plenty of customers who had no intention of purchasing an item have a change of heart when they picked it up, especially if the item was a plushy.

Booth layouts can be complicated and time-consuming to set up. Figures, wall scrolls, plushies, jewelry, key chains, hats and other disparate items all have different display requirements. You'll need to factor in the different shapes and sizes of your items and allow space for both the items and the corresponding displays within the boundaries of your booth.

You want to use every inch of the booth to your advantage. New vendors mistakenly leave too much empty space. They hesitate to rearrange the booth, preferring to squeeze their merchandise onto the table provided. But this leaves the majority of the booth empty. Customize your space in a way that works best for your merchandise. As long as the booth configuration meets your goal of displaying all of your merchandise that customers can easily see, you'll be in good shape.

Price signs, stickers and labels

Make sure the prices are clearly marked on all of your items. Customers prefer not to ask, 'How much?' And if you're busy when they want to know, they'll move on before they get an answer. Signs can also serve a purpose above and beyond informing people how much a single item costs. Customers decide to purchase multiple items much quicker if they can see the price versus having to ask. They know the actual cost and can calculate their total out-of-pocket expense immediately.

Do your best to make sure all prices and signage are printed from a computer. Handwritten signs scream, 'I'm willing to negotiate!' I also go as far as to include a color picture of the item next to its price on my signs. This alleviates any confusion about which price goes with which item and the signs look more professional.

Alas, a prominently-displayed sign doesn't eliminate customers looking directly at it and still asking the price. Use this question as an opening to boast about the uniqueness of your products and how they're only available in Japan. You may as well take the question as an invitation to talk profusely about your merchandise.

Security

It's worth giving a little thought to theft prevention when displaying items. The convention staff or the hotel will generally provide overnight security. They lock the dealer room during non-operational hours and vendors can only access the room during pre-determined time periods. Overnight theft rarely occurs, but if you have a $30,000 comic book – don't leave it in the dealer room overnight!

Theft primarily occurs when the dealer room is open and hundreds or thousands of attendees are roaming the aisles. Large conventions will have a separate security staff (mainly volunteers) patrolling the room but smaller cons may not. I have a small problem with one or two items developing legs and walking away at pretty much every convention. I'm a solo operator so when I'm busy helping customers, a *few* people will take advantage of the situation. Do your best to keep an eye on your booth and put your small, easy-to-pocket items out of reach.

Almost all dealer rooms are indoors but conventions held at botanical-garden-type locations will place the dealer's area in an open-air building or tent. Bring bug spray and a battery-operated fan, because it will be hot. The area will still have a roof overhead and some way to secure it overnight for multi-day events. You'll just have to cover your booth more securely overnight since the wind may knock things over.

Conventions are secure overnight and a little less so during operation, so plan for this. Big-ticket items should not be left overnight and easy-to-grab small items should be out of easy reach during business hours.

A BEHIND-THE-SCENES PEEK AT MY BOOTH

My booth setup (see below) includes the convention-provided table, a bench (6' x 2'), two fold out tables (4' x 4') and a myriad of supplies to prop up or hang up my merchandise. I am careful to choose supplies that are light, compact, portable and easy to transport.

The following pages feature close-up photos of the front, side and back of my booth taken at a few different conventions. Let's play 'Where's Waldo?' Can you spot all the display supplies?

9" x 5" x 5" cardboard boxes, 11" (H) and 21" (H) Styrofoam mannequin heads

Rotating necklace-display stand

SELLING TO HEROES, VILLAINS AND GEEKS

Spring clamps and straight sewing pins to attach items to drapes

Cardboard boxes, water bottles and doll stands

Doll stands, large boxes and acrylic price signs

Tablecloths covering booth when dealer room is closed

SELLING TO HEROES, VILLAINS AND GEEKS

The supplies I use for displaying items give my booth an inviting atmosphere. I want customers to feel free to touch and pick up the merchandise. Remember, once they are interacting with the items, they are more likely to purchase them.

 Sensei tip: Jewelry and accessory vendors should purchase a handheld mirror. Customers want to see how wearable items look on them. Attendees have numerous options, so make your booth as customer-friendly as possible. Always strive to make the buying process easy and enjoyable.

The most popular booth in the aisle

The best feeling in the world for vendors occurs when they see a line of people at their booth. You want to be so busy that eight hours fly by. Is this realistic? Absolutely! This happens all the time to vendors sporting merchandise that customers love. So, what are three display tricks of the trade that will draw a line of people to your booth?

The 'only a few left' trick

Don't put your entire inventory of any one item on display. This is the law of supply and demand we discussed in the psychology of pricing topic earlier. If you have twenty of the same item on display, people will question its popularity and exclusiveness. Consequently, potential buyers can lose interest.

If people see you only have one or two, they get nervous in a different way. They don't want to lose the item to someone else. When a customer asks me how many I have of a particular item, my answer is always 'two.' This creates a sense of urgency. Of course, we know that I have twenty more hidden under the table. Shhhhh!

The 'it has a special display therefore it must be popular' trick

How you display an item can be the difference between whether you sell twenty or zero. You can stock almost the exact same item as your competition and sell ten times more than they do. Why? Because prominently-displayed items garner more attention. And the right display increases the item's visibility, shows what the item actually looks like or its functionality, and triggers sales.

For example, *Dragon Ball Z* scouters are placed on mannequin heads in my booth. This display setup accomplishes three things. First, it helps customers to visualize the scouter on their face. Second, the scouters are easily spotted from the aisle. And third, it creates a lot of impulse purchases. Since other vendors keep the scouters in the box, I get one hundred percent of the convention's scouter business.

When a display helps customers visualize how it will look on them, they immediately want to see how it actually looks on them. And then they want their friends to take a picture. In this age of smartphones, selfies and social media, every fan is itchin' to take pictures of unique items that they can then share on Instagram. Oh yeah – when people ask to take pictures, say *yes!* Why wouldn't you want pictures of your booth and merchandise going viral? Or being shared among friends who are also at the convention? Taking pictures is also contagious. Often, people passing by stop to see what all the fuss is about and decide they also want to take a selfie with your merchandise.

People will also stand in my booth and text their friends a picture of an item. They'll sometimes get a quick text back asking their buddies to buy one for them. So, special displays, besides giving extra visibility to an item, also achieve a second goal of getting customers to interact with your merchandise and sharing photos among their friends.

The 'be the lucky one to find the buried treasure' trick

People like to rummage through bins in search of buried treasure. Customers (and there's no age limit here) are more than willing to sit on the floor and dig through piles of merchandise.

Once attendees start rummaging, they become emotionally connected to the search. This behavior is human nature. I can't explain it; I just capitalize on it. Veteran vendors spot this behavior and create displays to encourage it. For example, you'll see vendors throw dozens and dozens of shrink-wrapped posters in a large bin. Or you'll notice attendees patiently sort through a T-shirt vendor's rack of seventy-five different shirt designs.

However, this can be taken too far and quickly backfire. Comic book vendors often set out boxes containing 300 books in each. One vendor once went as far as to bring 10,000 comic books to a Comic Con convention.

10,000 comic books on display

Please don't go to this extreme. Take my word – this is a terrible idea. And I'm basing this on twenty-five years of experience in marketing. Nothing about a display with massive amounts of comic books makes the buying process easy for customers. Even the most die-hard comic book fans gave up on this vendor and sought out others with a more limited selection of books – 1,000 at most.

Okay, so you have a good head start now on what it takes to set up an amazing booth. Unleash your dormant interior design persona to perfect the optimal booth arrangement. There are countless ways you can design your booth, but if another vendor's layout fits your requirements, simply copy it. No need to reinvent the wheel if you find a perfectly good one.

Convention-goers walk up and down the aisles deciding which vendor merits a closer look. Your booth is your business billboard that will either grab their attention or go unnoticed. Whether the booth is elaborate or basic, your main goal is to showcase your merchandise and entice customers to stop and take a look. Now that we've discussed the best way to get customers to interact with your merchandise, we need to discuss the best way for you to interact with your customers.

THE MOMENT OF TRUTH

IMAGINE YOUR DAY STARTS OFF like this: You're all packed and ready to drive eight hours to a convention in its fifth year. Only twenty-two vendors are scheduled to participate so you're excited about the sales potential. Since attendance is projected at 2,000 people, you've decided not to rent a U-Haul trailer, managing to squeeze all of your gear inside the car while not blocking the side-view mirror. Yet, even with all of the planning and preparation you have done, you still wonder, 'Will I sell anything?' and 'Is this trip going to be worth it?'

After arriving at the convention, it's the moment of truth. The first sixty minutes after the doors open are always nerve-racking. If no one stops at your booth or you don't make a sale, don't worry. Depending on your booth location, it can take time for people to make their way around the dealer room at big conventions. Also, attendees like to window shop on the first day. The ebb and flow of conventions vary and a tortuously-slow morning can easily turn into a hectic, frenzied afternoon.

But, before you greet your very first customer, you need to decide on your customer service policy. 'What's to decide?' you ask. They want something and you sell it to them, right? Well, yes. But even so, almost every retail salesperson has completed a sales training program on how to approach customers and sell the company's products. And I'm guessing that most vendors don't have this formalized training. So we'll skip the four-week training program and just hit the critical things you need to know to ensure you have a positive interaction with your customers.

Even if you have amazing merchandise, it can make a big difference to your sales if you provide great customer service. Don't wince if your personality can hardly be described as outgoing. In fact, you can be quite shy. As long as the customer has a good shopping experience with you, they'll be very happy to tell their friends about your booth. So, what constitutes a good customer service policy? Let's find out.

Manage your customer service moments

'Can I buy this?' a customer asks you.

Surprisingly, you will hear this question multiple times during the convention. I find this hilarious and sometimes I answer 'no' just to see the customer's reaction. Convention-goers are polite and well-mannered. It's a pleasure to serve them. And remember, that is what you are there to do.

So be nice to your customers. I know, I know, this goes without saying. But I'm saying it anyway. It will make a difference to your sales.

Convention-goers enthusiastically talk to their friends about various vendors. They brag about what they bought, what other things the vendor was selling, whether they got a good deal and *whether the vendor was nice*. If the vendor was pleasant and let them take selfies with the merchandise even when they didn't buy anything, they often bring their friends back to that vendor's booth. The customer becomes an unpaid spokesperson. On the other hand, if the vendor was less than pleasant, the same attendees will urge their friends to avoid that booth like the plague.

 Sensei tip: Everything tastes better with honey. Being nice = $$$.

Now, 'be nice' is vague and subject to interpretation, so let me spell out what 'nice' looks like in your interactions with customers:

- If you only accept cash, *say it nicely with a smile*.

- If you don't want customers to touch items, *say it nicely with a smile*. Also, display a 'Please don't touch' sign next to those items.

- If you don't issue refunds, *say it nicely with a smile*. However, your 'no refund' policy should not apply to defective products. If a purchased item is ripped, doesn't work or is chipped – issue a refund.

- While your immediate reaction will be to deny a refund to someone who changes their mind (don't worry, this happens less than 0.003 percent of the time), issue a refund anyway. A no-hassle, no-questions-asked return policy works in your favor. Customers appreciate your flexibility and they will tell their friends that you are one of the 'nice' vendors.

- If a customer says, 'I have no money,' or 'If I had the money, I would definitely buy this,' don't shoo them away or ignore them. Let them hang out and dream about buying your merchandise. Why? First, you want other attendees to see people interested in your booth. Second, money has a funny way of raining from the sky – later in the day that same person will often purchase something. Third, you'll be labeled a 'nice' vendor once again.

- Show customers you care by discouraging them from using their food money to purchase an item when they say they are short on cash. They will appreciate you putting their health over you making a buck. But don't worry, you're not losing a sale – they'll spend the money at your booth anyway.

- Remind customers of any age restrictions on products if the final recipient is underage. A mother once insisted on buying a plushy for her eight-month-old son. I told her the recommended age for the product was three years and up but she blew off my advice and purchased it anyway. Point is, I showed I cared more about the customer than I did about selling one more item.

- Let kids and adults rummage through your bins in search of anime buried treasure even if they've already stated they have no money. I know they're taking up space in your booth, but you never know when that money cloud will blow in. I've let people rummage in my bins for over forty-five minutes at conventions. And I've lost count of how many times they return and buy an item from that bin, even if it's the next day.

- Be prepared to say, 'I'm sorry,' numerous times. Customers will ask, 'Do you have (fill in the blank)?' and if you don't carry the item, answer, 'I'm sorry, I don't carry it.' This response is more polite than just answering 'no.'

- If a customer asks you to hold a product until they come back, politely state you'll hold it for thirty minutes. Most of the time they return – but sometimes they don't.

- Smile... Even when a customer doesn't make a purchase, you still want to make a good impression. Customers sometimes window shop because they truly have no money for *this* convention. The next convention, however, they'll have money to burn and your booth will be their first stop.

You'll find the under-thirty-years-old crowd can't go home if they still have money remaining. You would swear the money is burning a hole in their pocket. When the last day of the convention rolls around, expect customers from the previous day to revisit your booth – especially if you've been nice.

 Sensei tip: Repeat customers are an excellent source of revenue on Sundays. Convention-goers want – no, *need* – to make one more purchase before the convention closes or life as they know it will come to an end. Vendors who treat them the nicest are their first stop. Give yourself an edge by treating all attendees, whether or not they make a purchase, with extreme kindness.

Customer service entails much more than just being nice, of course. For instance, make sure you have change available for your customers and also accept credit cards. This makes the purchase experience easy for them and it also prevents the purchasing process from short-circuiting due to a money issue. Prominently-displayed prices are also appreciated because they give the customer the information they need to make a prompt decision.

Customers will expect their items to be put in a thank you bag when they make a purchase. I'm constantly surprised by vendors who expect customers to purchase multiple items but don't provide a bag to carry it all in (I'm talking to you, Japanese snack vendors). Customers have backpacks, cosplay props, the convention program and other things in their hands. So, don't limit the number of items a customer will purchase by how many loose items they can carry – give them a bag. Doesn't this make good business sense?

Artists, take note. Don't sell a piece of artwork, sometimes for several hundred dollars, and just hand it to your customer *sans* bag, box or bubble wrap. Costco sells 1,000 bags at a cost of $0.02 each. This is a no-brainer. If I see an attendee walking around with a handful of items, I walk up to them and give them one of *my* thank you bags. You want to look after your customer.

When you deliver an enjoyable shopping experience the first time around for your customers or window shoppers, you increase their chance of coming back, time and time again.

So, you're all prepared and your booth is set up. You're in the zone for providing some great customer service. Let's see what a day (and another day and another day) at a convention is really like.

Good and bad convention moments

Let me share a day-by-day account of what vending at a convention will probably be like for you.

THURSDAY – THE DAY BEFORE THE CONVENTION OPENS

8:00 am	Load car, run through checklist and fill gas tank.

9:30 am	Depart for out-of-state hotel.

6:30 pm	Arrive at destination.

FRIDAY – OPEN FOR BUSINESS (FIRST DAY OF THE CONVENTION)

7:00 am	Arrive at convention site. Instructions state vendors must unload through loading dock. Convention has large handcarts for vendors. Yeah!

7:00 am – 8:00 am	Booths are not set up in the dealer room. Ugh! Convention service personnel arrive at 7 am to set up the booths. Wait, what? Personnel were previously informed by organizers they had from 7 am – 9 am to set up pipe and drapes. However, application states vendors can begin setting up at 7 am. Vendors sit around commiserating while service personnel erects pipe and drapes for every booth space.

8:05 am	Vendors begin setting up as soon as service personnel partly finish their area. Vendors step over pipes and drapes while carting inventory into room.

1:55 pm	(Heart-pounding, sheer panic begins to set in. Hoping, praying for a good day.)

2:00 pm	Dealer room opens for VIPs. There are very few VIPs waiting to get into room.

⌄

3:00 pm	Dealer room opens for all attendees.

⌄

8:00 pm	Dealer room is scheduled to close at 8 pm (per vendor application). Dealer room actually closes at 9 pm (the time printed in the official program). Wait, what? Vendors find out about the extra hour from convention staff at 8 pm.

⌄

9:00 pm	Dealer room closes. The staff remind vendors that doors open at 9 am Saturday. Wait, what? The application stated a 10 am start time. Sheesh! Daily sales are slightly below expectations.

SATURDAY – THE BIGGEST ATTENDANCE DAY

8:00 am	Arrive at convention hall. Uncover booth and restock merchandise on display.

⌄

8:55 am	(Pump up the energy level. Be pleasant and accommodating to everyone. Ready, set, smile.)

⌄

9:00 am	Dealer room opens (as per the time printed in the program not the application).

⌄

8:00 pm	Dealer room closes after eleven hours of operation – yikes! These long dealer-room hours are the exception, not the rule, for smaller conventions. Booth sales were brisk and met expectations.

SUNDAY – LAST DAY OF THE CONVENTION

9:30 am	Arrive at the convention hall. Uncover booth and restock display merchandise.

⌄

9:55 am	(Whatever, I'm tired, ready to break down, load up and head home.)

⌄

10:00 am	Dealer room opens.

⌄

3:00 pm	Some vendors start packing up already. Sales have been pretty slow all day.
	The staff inform vendors that load-out is a mere two hours, from 5 pm to 7 pm. Wait, what? That information was not included in the vendor application and two hours is uncharacteristically brief for vendor load-out.
	⌄
4:00 pm	More vendors start packing up to guarantee their exit from the convention center by 7 pm. More than half of the twenty-two vendors leave before the final hour (with the convention's permission).
	⌄
4:15 pm–5:00 pm	Sales take off at the few booths still open. Sold several hundred dollars' worth of merchandise. Yeah!
	⌄
5:00 pm	Dealer room officially closes.
	⌄
6:30 pm	Finally leave the convention. Good convention. Will attend next year.

 Sensei tip: Flying solo at your booth? Other vendors are always in search of more badges. In exchange for one of your extra badges, ask another vendor to periodically watch your booth while you take a three-minute break to grab some food or visit the restroom.

Vendors typically begin breaking down early on the last day since business and attendees are scarce in the final hours. The convention staff hates this but vendors don't want to sit around bored out of their skulls waiting for the convention to officially end. By this time, everybody is tired and a little cranky. And you still have to break down your booth, load up your vehicle and drive home. But the last hour of a convention can be a great opportunity for those last-minute, must-spend-my-money purchasers, so if you're packing up, don't look like you're closed for business.

The real moment of reckoning happens at the end of every convention when you determine how things went financially. Did you break even? Did you cover your expenses? Have you made a big profit? It's time to take a butt-naked assessment of the financial health of your vendor business.

SELLING TO HEROES, VILLAINS AND GEEKS

FINANCIALLY NAKED

CAN YOU HANDLE THE TRUTH, the whole truth, and nothing but the truth? It's time to talk profits, but this is not accounting advice (repeat after me the standard legal disclaimer to 'seek the opinion of a professional'). However, I'll dole out some basic tips and tools that will help you assess your financial success. You won't need an MBA or an in-depth understanding of double-entry accounting or anything like that. Earning profit can be as simple as acquiring items at the cheapest price and then charging the highest price most customers are willing to pay.

No one hits the ball out of the ballpark the first time at bat. It takes a few conventions to figure out the right mix of items. During your first couple of shows, you'll reconfigure your merchandise and restock with the bestselling anime and other items that customers frequently purchase. Identify inventory that's dead or moving slow and put those items on clearance so you sell them as fast as possible. That's right. Take the loss or lower profit margin and get them out fast. This will enable you to replace them with items that will make you more money.

The saying 'you win some, you lose some' does not apply to the vendor business. Outside of disastrous conventions that are ghost towns devoid of attendees, you should win them all. Maybe not by a lot – but you should be racking up financial wins at every convention. You'll need to calculate your financial health by putting together a profit and loss statement. This document lists your sales less your business expenses.

Two examples of a profit and loss statement for a convention may look like the following. In the "Breakeven" example, sales of $1,400 are needed to cover the convention costs. All sales above this can be considered a profit 'win!'

Profit and loss	Breakeven	Profit 'win'
Sales		$6,500
Cost of goods (50% of sales)	($700)	($3,250)
Gross profit	$700	$3,250
Expenses		
Vendor fee*	($400)	($400)
Hotel room (three nights)	($150)	($150)
Gas (round trip)	($90)	($90)
Parking	($30)	($30)
Food	($30)	($30)
Profit	$0	$2,550

*Vendor fee for one 10' x 10' booth

The assumptions used to calculate the profit in this example were:

- It's a non-local convention, hence the hotel room cost.
- You're transporting everything in your vehicle and not a rental.
- You have no employee costs (labor).
- Tax is not included in the sales figure. (Reminder: make sure you comply with all city and state sales tax laws to avoid serious penalties.)

The 'breakeven' sales figure is really a loss. How much time and effort have you put into that convention without making a dollar in profit? You are in this to make money.

Give yourself some financial flexibility by not counting on an upcoming convention to cover all of your outstanding bills. Over time, you'll work out which cons are right for you and how to achieve the best profits. But convention attendance can be erratic, so occasionally you'll just be happy to cover your expenses.

Profit 'wins' help to cover your initial investment (inventory, supplies, fees, and so on) and your ongoing business expenses (new inventory, supplies, future vendor fees, storage and more). Once you're racking up the sales, I'm sure you expect to make enough profit to contribute to other living expenses as well. It's a good idea to track your progress against the sales goal you set in your business battle plan so you can continually assess how your business is performing.

I know I don't need to say this, but larger conventions should be more profitable than smaller ones. Your bank account should be much fatter after vending at large conventions. I repeat, you should sell more merchandise – a whole lot more– at larger conventions than smaller ones. With five to ten times more people, your sales trajectory should ascend – it should not remain flat. Surprisingly, some new vendors don't pick up on this warning sign when their sluggish sales are the same at small and large conventions.

The road to financial success can be filled with New-York-sized potholes for new vendors. You need to know if you are only a few steps away from Brokesville.

The road to Brokesville

You can put lipstick on a pig, but it's still a pig. If you aren't making any profits, you're deluding yourself and are on your way to financial ruin unless you take immediate action.

Cute, but it's still a pig

Wipe every excuse from your lips. Excuses about light attendance, too many vendors, people having no money, the economy being bad, people saving for a rainy day, or the zombie apocalypse being upon us doesn't change the fact that you're not making a profit. Other vendors are profitable, so you can be too.

So, what do you do if you're constantly losing money?

Stop. Go directly to *Cardinal rule 1: Customer Con* if your sales do not deliver profit wins after a few conventions. It's time for a do-over. Completely toss your money-losing merchandise. Drastic? Yes! But you don't want to be that vendor – wedded to their merchandise and constantly losing money. Vendors who sleep in their van at every convention, by necessity and not by choice, desperately need a merchandise makeover. The van, in reality, is a hearse carrying their business.

 Oops alert: One new vendor was extremely happy with her sales at a convention. She confidently proclaimed this was one of her best shows yet. Over the two days she sold maybe $200 worth of merchandise. But she paid $175 for the booth space. Once you subtract the cost of the inventory, she actually lost money. Oh yeah, and I bought $60 worth of the merchandise she included in that figure since she always buys something from my booth. In short, she was in denial.

At conventions, I often see *former* vendors who lost money at every single show and consequently gave up vending. I always wonder what took them so long to realize they were on the road to Brokesville. But I also see *current* vendors who never have very many customers. They freely admit, 'We took a bath at XYZ convention.' Yet, here they are again, with the same merchandise, losing more money and leaving the convention early because they've sold nothing. I also repeatedly see artists in the vendors' area who barely sell five pieces of handmade items all weekend, if they're lucky. Frequently, they don't even make one sale and leave early. Like any new business, you can't jump in head first and hope for the best. Hope is not a strategy.

If it's broke, fix it – and fast. Waiting is not a financially-sound option.

One example of a first-time vendor who changed her merchandise mix to ramp up her sales is my friend Sydney. At her first convention, she brought her supply of figures she had accumulated over the years. They sold well enough but at bargain basement prices. As the convention wore on, she made mental notes of the other booths that were doing brisk business and what was selling well. She also asked me a hundred questions; we were booth neighbors, and that's how we became friends. She saw that plushies were selling like gangbusters and figures priced $20 to $60 from certain anime were selling out. My answers to her questions covered a lot of the information in this book. Sydney changed her merchandise to include popular plushies and higher-priced, unique and exclusive figures from Japan. Now, she is racking up profit 'wins' at every convention (and still asking questions to learn as much as possible – good for her!).

You have this book and the information and support you need to be a successful vendor. You are smart and special and want to learn. You've diligently studied and completed the assignments and created your merchandise and business battle plans. Your hard work has already radically improved your chance of success. You are armed with tools that no other new vendor previously had at their disposal. You've been schooled on how it works and what makes it work. You have insider knowledge, obtained legally. In fact, you're actually closer to being the exception – a new vendor who makes money at their first convention. Your future as an anime vendor is very bright.

If you've done your homework, your financial wins should pile up quickly. With all five cardinal rules in full force, your target customers will make a beeline to your booth. They'll spot the merchandise that appeals to them and you'll be giving out thank you bags with their purchased items in no time at all. To your delight, some customers who were intending to window shop will also spend money a lot earlier than they planned.

However, don't be tempted to rest on your laurels. Always be on the lookout for ways to refresh your inventory. New anime for each TV season are constantly premiering. You'll need to stay on top of unique or exclusive merchandise being churned out for popular anime shows. Stay alert. And plan on constantly testing new products to see if they sell.

If you have built your vending business based on the advice and ideas in this book, you have a great chance of running a successful business!

# Selling to Heroes, Villains and Geeks

THE FINALE

I really enjoyed writing *Selling to Heroes, Villains and Geeks* and I hope it dispensed way more information than you were expecting. We've taken quite a journey together. In *Part 1: The cardinal rules*, you were given the foundations upon which successful vending businesses are built. Then in *Part 2: Business battle plan blueprint*, you worked through your own plan of attack. We ended with *Part 3: Initiate launch sequence* and, hopefully, you're now imagining yourself standing in your amazing booth with your meticulously-researched, unique merchandise being fought over by a line of customers.

By working your way through all three sections, you have harnessed the know-how to get started and get it right. Could you still be feeling stuck on what direction to head in? Grappling with your business strategy? Probably not with all of the practical advice I've jam-packed into this book. But if you are, just read everything again and repeat every assignment. Also, talk to other artists and vendors who are successful. You'll be surprised how many are willing to give you helpful advice.

But wait! You have one last assignment. Before launching your business, ask yourself these questions:

1. Are you highly-organized?

2. Do you pay attention to the little details?

3. Is creativity a strong personal characteristic?

4. Do you like to learn new things?

5. Are you a people person (or can you at least fake it during convention hours)?

6. Do you believe patience is a virtue?

If you answered every question, 'Yeah, absolutely,' 'Indubitably,' 'Does the sun rise in the east and set in the west?' 'You betcha,' or 'Fo sho!' – then, you are ready! But will you succeed? Well, it's that old cliché: Nothing ventured, nothing gained. What's important is what you do next.

I hope there are scribbles, circles, arrows and to-do notes littering your notebook for *Selling to Heroes, Villains and Geeks*. This means you've done the work and you're on the fast track to launching your vendor business. But beware; there are no short cuts. You must follow the cardinal rules and then only make purchases in sync with your business battle plan. The magic formula for vending is a combination of hard work, research, creativity and patience. Use it to achieve the success you envision.

I hope to see you at a convention soon and, if you have a second, I would love to hear what you thought about this book. Please feel free to leave a comment on my website or drop me a quick note via email. Also, enter the code 'anime' on the 'Members' tab at animevendor.com for more behind-the-scenes information to grow your business. Definitely sign up for the bi-weekly emails to receive more sensei tips, oops alerts and new product updates. The emails will save you oodles of time on Google searches for the latest anime news.

Thank you for reading my book and I wish you nothing less than *super saiyan* success!

Jill Lewis

jill@animevendor.com

APPENDICES:

VENDOR'S GRAB BAG

APPENDIX 1: TRUSTED SUPPLIERS

Retail Japanese Websites		Comments
FromJapan	*fromjapan.co.jp*	Search engine and proxy purchasing service for all anime and manga products for sale in Japan.
Yahoo Auction	*auctions.search.yahoo.co.jp* (Proxy purchasing service agent required)	Largest Japanese auction site for arcade game and lottery prizes, and all products related to anime, manga and video games.
Rakuten Auction	*auction.rakuten.co.jp* (Proxy purchasing service agent required)	Auction site for anime and manga merchandise. Sellers charge higher prices than Yahoo auction sellers.
Amazon Japan	*amazon.co.jp* (Proxy purchasing service agent required)	The Japanese site for Amazon.

Retail Chinese Websites		Comments
Ibuyxyz	ibuyxyz.com	Occasionally, you can find good deals. A very limited number of anime series and merchandise categories sold.
Kakaanime	kakaanime.com PayPal address: kakaanime@yahoo.com Email address: kakaanime@hotmail.com	No minimum order. Can't pay directly from website store. Must submit payment separately through PayPal.
Wholesale Anime Merchandise Worldwide	myanimetoys.com	No minimum order.
You-Q	you-q.net PayPal address: cnyouq2@hotmail.com	No minimum order.
Crazy Anime Wholesale	crazyanimewholesale.com	$300 minimum order.
TAOBAO	taobao.com (Proxy purchasing service agent required)	Thousands of individual Chinese sellers. Must conduct product searches in Chinese. Do not use Taobao's proxy purchasing service. It's very expensive. Go to animevendor.com for video on how to conduct product searches on Taobao.
GE Yi Feng	Email and paypal address: mansun28@163.com	Chinese individual that provides all the services offered by a proxy purchasing service. This person charges 10% of the purchase price.

SELLING TO HEROES, VILLAINS AND GEEKS

APPENDIX 2: SAMPLE VENDOR APPLICATION

CONVENTION NAME

Date of Convention
EXHIBITOR CONTRACT
(Convention website address)
Exhibitor Room Hours
Friday: 2:00PM – 8:00PM, Saturday: 10:00AM – 8:00PM
Sunday: 10:00AM – 5:00PM
Exhibitor Room Setup: Thursday: 12:00PM – 8:00PM and
Friday 7:00AM – 1:00PM
Convention Location
Address

COMPANY: _____

NAME: _____

ADDRESS: _____

CITY: _____ STATE: _____ ZIP: _____

PHONE: _____

EMAIL: _____

WEBSITE: _____

Merchandise to be sold: _____

_____

_____

Are you interested in hosting any panels or events? If yes, provide the type of panel.

_____

_____

_____

CONVENTION RULES AND REGULATIONS

Please review the following rules and regulations governing the CONVENTION. If you have any questions or concerns, please contact us. By signing and returning the resulting contract, the EXHIBITOR confirms that they have read the following, agree to, and will comply with all rules and regulations as stated below.

1. All exhibitors and vendors must submit a signed copy of this contract. Email anyone@conventioncon.com, fax to (123) 456-7899 or mail to Convention 123 W. ABC Street, Any City, BL 23456. No exhibitor will be allowed to set up without submitting a signed contract.

2. Each space is 10' x 10' pipe and draped booth and comes with (1) 8 foot table, (2) chairs, (1) wastebasket and (2) exhibitor badges. (4 exhibitor badges for 2 booths and one extra for each additional booth.) Corner booths come with two tables: (1) 8 foot table and (1) 6 foot table. You may bring additional tables for your booth. Additional convention tables may be rented from the convention center at the event.

3. Exhibitors who arrive on Thursday (12:00PM – 8:00PM) or on Friday (7:00AM – 1:00PM) should check in at the exhibitor desk table by the loading dock. There will be no check in at the loading dock after 1:00PM on Friday. Anyone checking in late on Friday (after 1:00PM) must check in at the front registration desk for exhibitors and artists in the main lobby. Your booth assignment

will be confirmed before the event. All badges must be picked up at the show and will not be mailed prior to the event.

4. You may purchase additional exhibitor badges prior to the show for $35. Exhibitor badges are for exhibitors only and are not to be resold. Reselling exhibitor badges is a violation of the terms of this agreement.

5. All booths must be manned at all times. The CONVENTION will not be held responsible for any issues arising from an unmanned booth during show hours.

6. Booths must remain intact through the hours of the CONVENTION and may not be dismantled prior to the closing of the CONVENTION. The loading dock will not be open for breakdown prior to the close of the exhibition room. If you break down your space prior to the end of the show you will be banned from setting up at future shows. Attendees have paid for the ability to shop with vendors and exhibitors and expect them to be set up during show hours. By breaking down early you are doing both the attendees and the CONVENTION a disservice. Please be advised that there are vendors and artists that we will no longer welcome back due to breaking this rule. The CONVENTION management takes this very seriously. It is unfair to attendees, the CONVENTION and other vendors to break down early. If you cannot stay until the end of the show, please do not sign up for the CONVENTION.

7. Vendors and exhibitors will comply with all local, state and federal laws, and will not hold management liable for any breaches, losses, or damage to themselves or their property. All vendors and exhibitors agree to hold blameless the CONVENTION and all CONVENTION staff members and workers against any loss, damage, theft, expenses, claims or actions arising from any personal or property damage, loss or theft due to said vendors/exhibitors participation in the CONVENTION.

8. All vendors/exhibitors/artists acknowledge that CONVENTION and CONVENTION staff members, workers, employees and agents, will not provide or maintain insurance coverage for vendors/exhibitors, persons or property, and it is their sole responsibility to obtain insurance covering loss.

9. The CONVENTION in no way endorses any artists/vendors or exhibitor's merchandise, exhibits, views, beliefs and actions. All artists/vendors/exhibitors are deemed to be their own business/entity and in no way reflect the views, beliefs, and/or intentions

of CONVENTION. Artists/vendors/exhibitors do not represent CONVENTION in any way.

10. All merchandise bought or sold at the CONVENTION is done strictly between artists/vendors/exhibitors and attendees/buyers. The CONVENTION is not party to or responsible in any way for any transactions made between said parties.

11. All adult materials must be either behind the table or, if displayed on a table or display rack, bagged or covered so that minors may not open them. Any adult material containing nudity must be covered in accordance with local and state laws. Artists/exhibitors/vendors agree not to sell any adult materials to minors. Violating this rule is cause for immediate dismissal from the show with no refund, and being banned from any future events hosted by the CONVENTION.

12. No bingo or lottery type gaming (or gambling of any sort) is allowed.

13. No outside food vendors are allowed. The CONVENTION center has an exclusive on food sales. This applies to food trucks on CONVENTION center property. There is an exclusive vendor for this type of product.

14. State tax is the responsibility of the exhibitor/artist/vendor to collect, according to state laws.

15. No bootleg DVDs or CDs. Representatives from various studios will be at the convention. Anyone selling unauthorized merchandise that infringes upon their copyright or licensing agreements (or any other studio's copyright) will be asked to leave the show. No refunds will be given if you break this rule and are asked to leave.

16. Electrical service for your booth is available directly from the CONVENTION center via their website at electricalserviceorderform.com. At the show, electrical services will be available from the CONVENTION center at a much higher rate.

17. Wireless internet is available from the CONVENTION center at the event. The order form is at the end of this packet.

18. Parking at the CONVENTION center is $10 per day (with no in/out) or $15 per day (includes in/out).

19. No exhibit may block or interfere with other exhibits or with the aisle space. Any damage caused to the building or its furnishings by artist/exhibitor/vendor are the sole responsibility of the artist/exhibitor/vendor.

20. Should the artist/vendor/exhibitor find that they are unable to attend the CONVENTION and have already paid for their space, the policy is as follows: A refund will be given (minus $XX cancellation fee) prior to cancellation by X date. No refunds will be made after X date.

PRICING AND AVAILABILITY

Pricing and availability are as follows:

Corner booth: $500. These corner spaces have two edges facing into the room, and thus allow for maximum display space.

Inner booth: $400. These spaces have one edge facing the room, and are located in the center of the dealer's room.

BOOTH SPACE
(see map on website for available booth numbers):

Number of booths required: _____

Booth number(s) _____

HOURS OF OPERATION, SETUP AND TAKE DOWN:

Hours of operation for the dealers' room are as follows:

Thursday:
- 12:00PM – 8:00PM: setup for vendors

Friday:
- 7:00AM – 1:00PM: setup for vendors
- 2:00PM – 3:00PM: dealer room open to VIP ticket holders
- 3:00PM – 8:00PM: dealer room open to all attendees

Saturday:
- 9:00AM – 10:00AM: setup for vendors
- 10:00AM – 11:00AM: dealer room open to VIP ticket holders
- 11:00AM – 8:00PM: dealer room open to all attendees

Sunday:
- 10AM – 5:00PM: dealer room open to all attendees
- 5:00PM – 10:00PM: vendor breakdown

All exhibitors must be show-ready a minimum of 60 minutes prior to exhibit hall opening.

Method of payment:

Online payment/check/money order (made payable to the CONVENTION)

Send payment to: CONVENTION 123 W. ABC Street, Any City, BL 23456 or pay online at conventioncon.com

Registration is complete after receipt of payment and contract.

I understand and agree to the terms of this contract.

Signature _____

Date _____

ILLUSTRATION AND PHOTO CREDITS

		Page/Location
Cover Art	© Robert Chang *ethereality.info*	Front Cover
Design	Scarlett Rugers Design *scarlettrugers.com*	Front Cover, Spine, Back Cover, Interior
Author portrait	© Michael Lenehan *mick2006.deviantart.com*	2
Photo	Artist Table by John P. Alexander Krystal Alexander (pictured) *lexlothor.deviantart.com*	8
Photo	Lilla Eros (purple costume) - pictured; Photo by Christian Flierl *facebook.com/cyrencosplay*	28
Photos	L.A.E. cosplay photography *laecosplayphotography.com*	21, 43, 49, 50, 51

HONORABLE MENTIONS

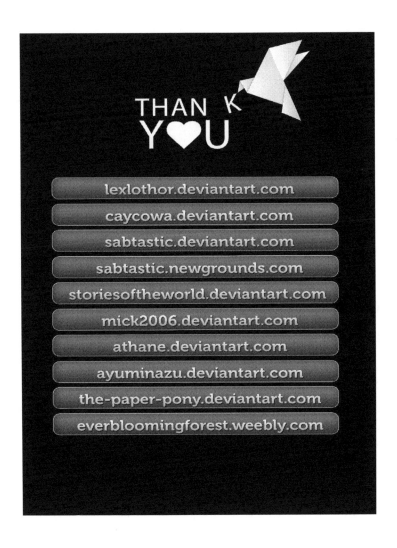

THANK YOU

- lexlothor.deviantart.com
- caycowa.deviantart.com
- sabtastic.deviantart.com
- sabtastic.newgrounds.com
- storiesoftheworld.deviantart.com
- mick2006.deviantart.com
- athane.deviantart.com
- ayuminazu.deviantart.com
- the-paper-pony.deviantart.com
- everbloomingforest.weebly.com